Soul Speak

Opening to Divine Guidance

Soul Speak

Opening to Divine Guidance

Cheryl Stoycoff

Living Spirit Press

Manufactured in the United States of America
Library of Congress Catalog Card Number: 00-90045
ISBN: 0-9677852-0-0
Author's photo by Wendy Gritsch
Cover design: Osprey Design Systems, Inc.
Book design and production by Tabby House

Publisher's Cataloging in Publication
(Provided by Quality Books, Inc.)

Stoycoff, Cheryl
    Soul speak : opening to divine guidance /
Cheryl Stoycoff. -- 1st ed.
    p. cm.
    Includes biographical references
    LCCN: 00-90045
    ISBN: 0-9677852-0-0

    1. Parapsychology. 2. Psychic ability
3. Channeling (Spiritualism) 4. Spiritual life--New
Age movement.   I. Title.

BF1031.S76 2000   133
                              QB100-262

Living Spirit Press
Books for an Awakening Consciousness
P. O. Box 70214
Stockton, CA 95267
E-mail: livingspirit@cherylstoycoff.com
Internet Web Page: http://www.cherylstoycoff.com

Acknowledgments

NO ONE IS ALONE. So many others help us as our soul grows to know itself. I would like to acknowledge all those who have helped me in my search for answers: the authors whose books opened my eyes, the visionaries of history who paved the way for enlightenment in a darkened consciousness, and the clients who have allowed me the grace to teach them and in doing so provided me the means to learn. I am eternally grateful for the presence of love that the earth knows as Jesus and for this guidance in my life. This love has allowed me to understand, to grow and to evolve.

My thanks goes to Wendy Gritsch for her constant support, pure heart and unending friendship. And to Clyde Stoycoff, my husband, who provided unending support, honest and loving criticism, hours of editorial and administrative work and always saw the light within me, even when I didn't. He has shared this vision and has lived this truth as I have, throughout our many lifetimes together.

Dedication

To my soul mate, Clyde, whose unending love
and support helped me find the light within.
And to Zack and Kyle, two beautiful souls,
who shine so brightly in my life.

Contents

Part III
Experiencing

Appendix

Introduction

Soul Speak is about discovering and experiencing the untapped potential within yourself. The ability to feel as others feel, to perceive beyond the usual five senses, to understand your existence and to tap into the answers and guidance, you need to grow spiritually.

There is so much untapped within us. So many people are searching for what they intuitively know is there, unable to put the quest or destination into words, but feeling that internal pull toward the unknown that is our destiny to experience.

As I type these words, I feel the familiar pulsating energy in my solar plexus, a constant reminder of the connection between the world we see every day and the world we cannot see. I reach within, pulling through feelings and emotions to help you understand what you hold within. I stumble as I try to interpret these into words. There are no words that can do justice to the depth of understanding available to you, once you have the direct experience of your soul.

As you read these pages, you will recognize yourself, because your soul is searching, pulling you forward, urging you to discover what it already knows. There is an infinite potential that lies dormant within you. It has only been covered up, inaccessible, through our living in unnatural ways, through centuries of programming, through society's structures that we took on as our own and through inaccurate perceptions from our parents and peers regarding who and what we are. Our bodies have become clogged, our perceptions clouded and our energy centers blocked. As a result, we are no longer able to feel our inner connection, a connection that is as natural and necessary to our spirits as breathing is to our bodies.

Through the activation of my Kundalini, I now experience the psychic gifts of clairvoyance, clairaudience and clairsentience. I experience a constant, open channel to the world that exists beyond our physical world. Through this channel, I am able to draw forth information, knowledge and wisdom to assist myself and others on our spiritual paths. This connection has served to alter my perception of myself and the world to allow for a continual experience of communion with the Divine Source. Daily, I am in awe of our connection. These intuitive abilities that have been opened within me continue to show me there is no separation between us. I feel your feelings and I experience your thoughts. I literally feel our connection daily and it is my wish for you to feel it too.

I have always felt that this is a natural process, something we are all meant to experience. As the changes occurred within my body and mind, I was able to observe the process unfolding, revealing to me, through my direct experience, those obstacles that serve to keep us blocked. As my perceptions expanded, my body changed. My channels opened and my energy blocks were released. Each step cleared the way for a stronger experience of the Divine Source within. It became apparent to me how and why we are not able to feel and directly experience our connection to the whole. In understanding this process and making the mental and physical changes that allow for a return to balance and harmony, you can tap into the Divine Source that is your essence. I have written this book to share with you what is possible so you will expand your paradigms and open to experience more of yourselves. There is so much available to you. Your potential is only limited by the reality you have chosen to experience. This book is divided into three parts. The first takes you through my experiences as they happened. This was a time of great discovery for me. Thus, I call Part I "Discovery." I have included as much detail as possible, yet, I know that with some of my experiences, even the most carefully chosen words will not do justice to the intense feelings and realizations I experienced. I feel the inclusion of this personal information is necessary for you to understand the process of unfoldment which occurs as we open to experience the larger part of ourselves.

In Part II, I have shared with you the insights and explanations I received in my attempt to understand what was happening to me. These are the experiences that helped me put together the pieces, allowing me to integrate this new reality into my life. There are many things to absorb and many new concepts to understand. Since this was a time of trying to integrate and understand, I have called Part II "Understanding."

Part III, is titled "Experiencing." The information included in this section will assist those who are ready to experience their own connection. I have provided practical and detailed guidance to help you unblock your energy centers, purify your body, expand your perceptions and integrate your emerging spirituality into your daily life. These practices, combined with earnest intent and true desire for Divine communion, are the keys to opening to Divine guidance and directly experiencing your soul.

As you read these pages, let go of your current perceptions and try to stretch your limits. Let go of feelings of fear or inadequacy and open your heart. It is through your heart that you will be able to make the switch and overcome the logical mind that holds you within the accepted structures. It is through your heart that you will be awakened. As you begin to feel with your heart, you will be able to proceed with the process of opening your consciousness and you will directly experience what you truly are, a spiritual being in a physical body. Come with me now, let me take you where I have been so you can experience the wonder of yourself.

CHERYL STOYCOFF
STOCKTON, CALIFORNIA

Part I

Discovering

*Miracles happen, not in opposition to nature,
but in opposition to what we know of nature.*
—St. Augustine

CHAPTER 1

Kundalini

WITH A JOLT, I AM AWAKENED as it shoots through me, arching my back, expanding and pushing my chest into the air as if a hook were embedded in my sternum and was pulling me upward. I breathe in deeply, air filling my lungs from the bottom up, then exhaling. I feel a familiar peacefulness engulf me as my body relaxes and waits for the next surge. I glance at the clock, 2:00 A.M. I say to myself, "Right on schedule."

My mind settles into that familiar expanse, void of thought activity and mental grasping. I feel the rush again, building in my tailbone and pushing its way upward, through my spine, expanding my midsection and lifting my body into a rhythmic spasm as my muscles tense in automatic response. Again, I exhale and relax into the peacefulness.

I feel a deepening within; my body seems to sink into the bed and everything seems to move out of time, as if I am in suspended animation. The energy pulse begins more slowly this time, moving upward, more deliberately now. This time, there is no crescendo in my chest; instead, the pulse travels upward, through my body, into my head. I feel a tingling and expansion in my brain. I relax further, letting nature take its course. There is more tingling in my head, centralized in the center, just behind my forehead. It feels like millions of nerve endings are moving, spreading out, intertwining and multiplying. I experience a feeling of further expansion and the sense that there are physiological changes taking place, changes that I cannot explain, yet I know there is no need for concern or panic. Deep within there is a knowing that this is a natural phenomenon, a transition of my body, a transition that is taking me into new realms of human evolution.

Ever since man appeared on the earth there has been within us the burning question of our origin. At some point throughout our lives some event will serve as a catalyst for our search to answer the question, "Who am I?" It is this question that drives us on, sending us searching our spirituality, exploring our religions and analyzing our beliefs. Our ability to sense the answers to this question is heightened and our resources to understand the answers are expanded. We embark on a spiritual journey. This searching usually begins around midlife, usually between the ages of thirty-five and forty and continues until our physical death.

As we search for answers, many things are revealed to us and our understanding expands. It is our seeking that draws to us what we need for further understanding and opens our perceptions. Just as a bird knows where to fly for the winter and the whale knows its migratory route, we are likewise driven instinctively toward our goal of spiritual evolution. There is an inherent force within us, awakening from its dormancy to drive us forward in our search for answers in an attempt to experience the ultimate goal of our soul—union with the Divine.

We turn to our religions because that is where we have been taught to look for the Divine, but are often disillusioned as our thirst for direct experience is not fulfilled. The promise of communion with the Divine after our physical death is not enough when we sense that so much more than words are available to us now. Often, we turn from religion, taking what we can from it and begin to create our own spirituality—that is not based on words or doctrines, but is based wholly on our inner knowing of what will bring to us the direct experience we seek and intuitively know is there.

As we continue our search we find answers coming to us in many forms and we begin to understand the nature of the universe, through our own experiences. This is how we evolve. It is this experience the soul craves, to know itself in its true form, that of a Divine being, while holding awareness in a physical body. As the drive within us becomes stronger, we will draw to ourselves many experiences that allow for the understanding of our true nature. As we put together the pieces, many things are revealed to us and we begin to understand our path and the reasons for our lifetime's experiences.

Within us lies the key, an untapped energy, which, when activated, provides the physical link to our origin as a Divine being. Once this energy is activated within the body, a cycle of changes begins to happen to our physical body, allowing for the union of physical matter and the pure energy that pervades everything in existence. We experience a union with our Divine soul.

This untapped energy is known as Kundalini and is the driving force behind our search. The energy that is Kundalini is still a mystery to our logical minds. It cannot be seen or measured. Once activated, one loses all desire to analyze it or logically understand it and therefore there remains much mystery surrounding it, what initiates its activity and how we can control it. Carl Jung, in *Psychological Commentary on Kundalini* said that, "When you succeed in awakening the Kundalini, so that it starts to move out of its mere potentiality, you necessarily start a world which is totally different from our world. It is the world of eternity."[1] Gopi Krishna, inspired by his own experience of Kundalini awakening, has written much to describe its meaning. He says of Kundalini, "A new center presently dormant in the average man and woman has to be activated and a more powerful stream of psychic energy must rise into the head from the base of the spine to enable human consciousness to transcend the normal limits. This is the final phase of the present evolutionary impulse in man . . . Here reason yields to intuition and revelation appears to guide the steps of humankind . . .This mechanism, known as Kundalini, is the real cause of all genuine spiritual and psychic phenomena, the biological basis of evolution and development of personality, the secret origin of all esoteric and occult doctrines, the master key to the unsolved mystery of creation . . . "[2]

The very nature of the Kundalini is energetic. It has intelligence, yet not as we understand the word. There is no reasoning or calculation. There is no manipulation or premeditation. There is only pure response, pure awareness seeking out that which will satisfy its reason for existence. This force that ties us to our energetic origin lies within our root chakra at the base of our spine. (See Appendix for an explanation of the Chakra System.) As we actively begin to seek answers to our spiritual questions, the power of our thoughts and intent serve to activate a stirring of this energy within us. The more intense our desire for union becomes, the more the Kundalini stirs. When we have grown enough in our understanding and trust enough in our inner guidance, we open ourselves to the direct experience that awaits us. The Kundalini begins its ascent up through our Chakra System, from the base of the spine to the crown of the head. This ascent can take many lifetimes, many years or many months. Each one is unique and no two are alike. Although there is a pattern of sequence that the Kundalini follows, its speed depends on many factors that vary from soul to soul.

There is no prior knowledge needed to activate the Kundalini. Even though there are many people who follow a precise set of practices, especially in eastern cultures, to activate the Kundalini, no knowledge is necessary. This is a natural stage of our evolution. Just as nature takes over when a mother gives birth, it emerges when it's ready and continues to fulfill its Divine purpose, regardless of our knowledge or understanding of the process.

This is the experience I will share with you. When my Kundalini first activated, I had no idea what was happening. I didn't know it had a name or that it was being experienced by many people as we enter the new millennium. I only knew that I was driven on by my desire to understand and know more and what I experienced only whetted my appetite to further merge with this energy that had so profoundly changed my reality. At times it has seemed so personal that I could not speak of it, but as it grew within me and I expanded and experienced what lies beyond my physical mind, the perception of myself as separate from you has changed. I no longer feel as though I am speaking to other individuals. The sharing of my experience is simply you, drawing to yourself what you need to grow and expand. We are one.

CHAPTER 2

The Energy

M Y DISCOVERY OF THIS ENERGY that pervades everything and connects us to each other was due to my searching for relief from the world in which I did not fit. I have found, through my intuitive sessions, that this feeling is shared by many and is being accelerated in recent years. I will share with you what precipitated the awakening of my Kundalini so that you will recognize yourself and understand where your own experiences and difficulties are ultimately leading you.

Initially, I had begun to meditate as a way of reducing stress. I had always been a Type A personality, a depression-prone perfectionist who was always discontented on some level, regardless of my circumstances. My nervous system seemed too sensitive for the world in which I found myself. Physically, my body overreacted to medications, alcohol and extreme changes in temperatures. Emotionally, I was sensitive to a fault. Tears sprang to my eyes as I viewed the suffering of the world, feeling the pain and emotions of others as though they were my own. I was notorious for crying at movies, to songs on the radio, even television commercials! My sensitivity made for a hard life as I tried to make sense of the world which I felt so strongly all around me. By the time I was thirty-four, I had developed a severe case of TMJ[3]. I was unable to open my mouth wide enough to brush my teeth and I feared I would have to eat through a straw for the rest of my life. After medical science and modern dentistry were unable to offer any solutions, I took up yoga to learn meditation in an attempt to relieve stress and reduce the severity of the TMJ. Through meditation, I learned there was a whole inner world I had not previously allowed myself to discover. I also found that in focusing on this inner world my "issues" came to the surface. Those painful memories that I had avoided all my life kept cropping up. It became apparent that my pattern of always having to have my mind occupied and always having to be doing several things at once was actually a way of keeping myself from turning my focus inward, where these painful feelings would have to be dealt with.

Meditation awakened a searching within my soul and a transformation began to take place. I began to explore various holistic therapies and alternative viewpoints to organized religion. I became a vegetarian and began studying for a degree in holistic nutrition. This is what lead me to discover Reiki, an ancient Tibetan healing art similar to the laying on of hands, and initially experience the energy. I was doing research for a paper on alternative therapies and I attended a workshop given by a Reiki Master[4] with the intention of gathering enough information to complete my paper. I sat there, rather skeptically, waiting for the demonstration. You could have pushed me over with a feather when the woman behind me placed her hands above my head and I actually *felt* something! I vowed to receive the Reiki Attunement[5] myself as soon my finances would allow. I was definitely intrigued and anxious to feel more of this energy. I wanted to understand exactly what it was and how it worked.

I scheduled my attunement for the following January, about four months away. I was very anxious and the time passed slowly. My meditation increased during this time because I felt something special was going to happen. I didn't know what, but I knew somehow my life would be different.

At the attunement, I waited anxiously for my turn. I wasn't sure what to expect, but I had a kind of "knowing" within that

I was exactly where I was supposed to be. After the attunement was performed, I was able to feel the energy flowing through my body and out through my hands. This was much more intense than I had felt at the workshop. I experienced the energy as a "filling up" from the inside. My solar plexus area would expand and I would feel my heart beat intensely within the center of the energy. My hands would throb and tingle and then would become very warm when the energy was flowing. In addition, my body would heat up, much like a hot flash. I thought I must be very sensitive to the energy, because I felt a very intense "centralizing" of it, as if I had taken a lot of caffeine. (I later learned this was my body's energy centers opening to accept and channel the energy.)

The following explanation, which came to me as I searched for answers, will further explain this energetic source for all of life: To understand what is possible and what you are capable of, you must first understand that everything is energy. There are ninety-two elements found in nature. An atom is the smallest unit of an element known to exist. The atoms that we are made of are the same particles that form the entire universe. Science has told us that if you break down the smallest measurable part of the atom, matter dissolves into electrical energy. This energy is the basis of all life. This is the energy that flows through our bodies, through the planets, the stars and all of creation. This point of energy that is found at the point where energy becomes matter is where science has abandoned its search for understanding, because the energy cannot be measured or seen. It can be felt, however, and it is through this feeling that we may learn more about ourselves and all of life.

If we take up where science has left off and explore this energy through the part of ourselves that is untouched by science and intellect, we can directly discover that this energy is the source of creation and continues to run through each one of us, connecting us to everything, in a very real, tangible way. The energy does not subside when it slows its vibration to create the atom, nor when the atoms join together to form molecules, nor when the molecules join together to form cells. At the heart of each atom is a nucleus and orbiting around each nucleus are protons, neutrons and electrons. The speed at which the protons, neutrons and electrons orbit within the atom can also be described as the energy vibration of that atom. When it is said that you are "vibrating at a different level," this is literally true, as the density of the organic matter which makes up your body is changed molecularly by the very atoms that comprise the cells of your body.

Now, let's return to the energy. Just as the energy becomes matter in the form of the atom which comprises the human body, so it is with everything in existence. The matter which makes up the planet also begins as energy, as the vibration is slowed and an atom appears, physical matter is formed. Every element found in the earth has at its core the same atom, comprising dense energy, that we do. The only difference is the way in which the atoms have joined together to form various organic substances. Energy is the common thread that connects us to each other, to all plant and animal life, to the planet and beyond. At the energetic level, we are all the same ONE. It is important to understand that this energy that can be felt and interpreted as being "of spirit" is not something that exists outside of your physical body, it is not "other than" you. The energy did not cease when the atom appeared as physical matter. You are this energy, only the form (the vibration) of the energy has changed.

The experience of energy running through my body began to transform me. I sought out information to understand it more fully. It was intensifying and I realized my mind was trying to keep up with what my body was experiencing. I began to read everything I could find to help me understand this force I was experiencing.

Spirit

IN MY RESEARCH, I WAS INTRIGUED by the idea of spirit guides. These are beings who are no longer in physical bodies and are with us to assist us along the spiritual journey of our soul. I found that the energy was actually leading me to what would answer my questions. As I browsed in a bookstore, I would pick up a certain book and feel an immediate increase in the energy fluttering in my solar plexus. I would pick up a different book and feel nothing. I allowed this guidance to direct me to what I needed to learn. In this way, I was led to books about contacting your spiritual guides and even channeling them to access guidance directly. This was definitely the direction I was being driven toward. I read all I could find on these subjects.

At this time in my life, I was desperately looking for "my path." I was unhappy with my job at an insurance agency (my career of fifteen years prior to my awakening). I had always felt as if I didn't fit and found it hard to stay with any job for too long due to feelings of being unsatisfied and feeling that I needed to search, but for what I did not know. I needed some direction. I had always felt there was something I was supposed to do. I was always a little different due to my sensitivity, yet I didn't know why I felt that way. I thought my path may have something to do with Reiki, because I had such a strong reaction and acceptance of the energy. This was my motivation for wanting to contact my guide. I wanted direction and if he could help me, I was ready to listen. I had spent long enough doing things that did not feel important to me. I knew there was something more. I yearned to fill my days with something that was valuable to mankind, something that would make a real contribution. More than that, I wanted to enjoy what I did each day.

I know many of you struggle with these same feelings. You feel trapped in the same job, feeling you are unable to make a change. You feel trapped for financial reasons. You have family that depends on you and you cannot see a way out. You will learn, as I did, that you are very able to make a change and it is much easier than scouring the want ads for job listings. You will learn to make the changes you want, the changes your higher-self wants you to make, and these changes will flow effortlessly. When you look to change the *external*, the house, the job, the relationships, you are only changing the packaging. What is inside remains the same. These external changes will manifest themselves as a natural extension of the changes you make *internally*. When you change the contents, the packaging has to come off and then be replaced.

When I was ready to contact my spiritual guide, to find out if it was true, if it was possible and what it meant to my life, I was directed to the book *Opening to Channel* by Sanaya Roman and Duane Packer (H. J. Kramer, 1987) and immediately began to follow the guidelines it gave.

On the day of the Kundalini activation, I began meditating as usual and reached the place of "no-mind," the place between the thoughts. As I mentally asked for a guide, I opened my body through relaxation to feel the response. As I did this, I felt energy come into my body and completely fill me. It kept filling me up, expanding me outward like a balloon. I felt as though my middle would burst! My breathing became deeper and I was aware of the most exquisite feeling of love, peace and joy. I felt as if I were being bathed in it. There are no words to explain how wonderful this felt. I remember thinking that this must be what "the light" feels like, the place people describe when they have had a near-death experience. I was completely surrounded and immersed in this feeling of joy and love. The presence of the energy I felt was so wonderful, so loving, I did not want it to leave. I felt no fear. Even though what was happening seemed quite extraordinary to my logical mind, somewhere deeper I knew it was natural and was not so extraordinary.

The weeks that followed brought more of the same. Intense energy flowed through me each time I relaxed my body. I existed on little food and did not seem to need much sleep. During the night it seemed to be most intense, when my body was the most relaxed.

Several months after that first experience, in searching for an explanation, I learned there was a name for what was happening to me. I had experienced the awakening of my Kundalini. This transformational spiritual energy consciousness that was previously dormant had awakened within me and had set in motion an intense spiritual transformation, catapulting me toward discovery, acceptance and integration with the Divine Source. There is no translation in our western world that adequately describes the totality of the spiritual awakening in one's life once the Kundalini has been activated. It is indeed impossible to doubt that the connection to a Divine Source is within each one of us, once you have felt its physical presence and direction within your body.

I have read that serious seekers strive for years to activate the Kundalini, undertaking ambitious meditation practices, bodily cleansing rituals and often traveling to distant lands to seek assistance from spiritual masters. How was it that I, a middle class, thirty-something wife, mother and insurance secretary with no spiritual or metaphysical background, found myself experiencing such phenomenal things? Within a matter of days, I was catapulted from my "normal" everyday life to experiencing incredible psychic phenomena, receiving clairvoyant images, communicating with spirit, seeing auras, reading energy patterns and experiencing past life regressions. I was thrown into a whole new world that I never knew existed and that I previously didn't even believe in!

Through all the extraordinary experiences that have come to me, I have found one simple truth to be the explanation for everything that has happened; we are all quite literally *one being.* The connection we share is beyond this physical world. It is *before* this physical world. It is vitally important for us to dissolve our perception that we are separate from each other, our perception that we are separate from other forms of life, our perception that we are separate from the earth, our perception that our minds are separate from our bodies and our perception that our spirituality is "other than" our physical existence. It is clear to me that in order to become whole, to achieve the healing that the world is currently seeking, we must be able to experience directly, within ourselves, our connection. This direct experience will automatically change our perceptions of what and who we are and, therefore, our perception of separation.

It is this direct experience that we are meant to feel. It is the way we are meant to live. Life is not meant to be a struggle. We are not meant to wander in despair and confusion, our bodies numbed out with medications and addictions. We are meant to experience the divinity of ourselves, through our physical bodies, and to experience the expansion of our awareness and the joy of these new discoveries, every day of our lives.

These truths are simple and they are meant for everyone to know directly, from within. When we become whole and align with our true selves, all is revealed and everything that was ever sought suddenly becomes clear. Your mind is the manifestation of the creative power of the universe, which resides within you. Your body is the vehicle which enables you to experience this Divine presence that is your soul.

During the weeks that followed the initial opening, I found myself exploring many possibilities, or explanations for what I was experiencing. I knew what was happening to me was real. I had always been a pragmatic person and I needed to explain my experiences in logical terms. Truthfully, I found this approach to be a hindrance to my growth. Although my logical mind continued to look for tangible, scientific ways these things could be explained, I found I was relying more and more on my intuition, or sixth sense, for guidance and understanding.

The things that were unfolding before me changed the very nature of what I thought to be true and what I thought to be important. I had to question the things I always took for granted, things that had been conditioned into me from birth. I questioned the beliefs of our society regarding what is possible and what is nonsense or fantasy. Because of what I was experiencing, I was becoming a different person, with new beliefs, new ideas and an expanded awareness of what constitutes reality.

CHAPTER 4

Accessing

A S I DESCRIBE WHAT OCCURRED over the next few weeks, it is important to keep an open mind. These things will sound unbelievable to some, for just as I was unaware of the existence of these things prior to my experiences, there are many who doubt the existence of that which they cannot see or touch. If you find yourself in this company, I challenge you to reach out with your feeling center, to close your eyes and discover what you feel. You will find there are many things that we trust on feelings alone and these things give us the greatest pleasure and the richest experiences.

There may be some who have experienced similar things, but could not explain what was happening to them. In many cases, these individuals close themselves off, choosing to suc-cumb to their fear of the unknown. They choose to "play it safe" and discontinue their journey because it is foreign to them. If you recognize yourself here, you are missing perhaps the best part of yourself. If we do not stretch our boundaries, and reach for the unknown, no growth will be found. When the pioneers in our history ventured into unknown territory, they risked upsetting what they thought to be true. If not for this natural, human trait, there would be no discoveries, no technological advances, no new territories or planets explored.

From this perspective, there is no harm in exploring what is unknown to us, in taking a look at it, in seeing for ourselves and in trying to understand something new. We are an intelligent species, able to use logic and reason to understand things. We also possess capabilities that are not as well developed. These capabilities are within every one of you: the ability to sense subtle things around you; the ability to just *feel* if something is right. The ability to just *know* something, even without what the world would consider "proof." The ability to hear something and somehow realize that within it lies truth, even if you can't logically explain it. We have all been taught to disregard these things, taught not to trust our feelings, taught not to trust ourselves, especially if it goes against what society considers normal. It has been a hard lesson for me to learn these things. I have had to face many fears and doubts from myself as well as others.

After the initial opening, my meditation took on a new focus. I was determined to have more contact with my guide and I wanted to hear what he had to say to me regarding my path. I was open to whatever assistance he could give. I began to request that he come closer because I wanted to hear him more clearly and to communicate with him openly. Each time I would meditate, I would feel his energy surround me and it felt wonderful. I would emerge from my sessions feeling very peaceful and full of love. I began to ask for what I wanted. Some would call it praying, but this was a foreign concept to me. I worded my requests respectfully, asking for guidance, stating that I wanted to know what I was to do. I asked for signs and signals that would lead me where I was to go.

Soon thereafter, as I sat meditating, I realized I felt the energy around me much stronger than I had before. I felt it was my guide and asked him to fill me with more energy and I mentally opened myself to receive this energy. I relaxed my body and waited. Suddenly, I felt a *swoosh* run through me. I felt energy come into my body and completely fill me up. It kept filling me up as though my middle would burst. Simultaneously, my breathing became deeper, my back arched, my head was thrown backwards and my chest was thrust forward.

I was aware of the most exquisite feeling of love, peace and joy. I felt as if I were being bathed in it. There are no words to explain how wonderful this felt. I was completely surrounded and immersed in this feeling of joy and love. I mentally asked, "Who are you?" and I received a mental answer, "Ramsey." I wish to convey that even though this was something totally new to me, I was in no way afraid. The presence of the energy I felt was so wonderful, so loving, I did not want it to leave. Before the energy dissipated, I mentally spoke to Ramsey. I requested direct guidance for my path and I requested more communication. I wanted to understand what had happened to me and I wanted to be able to control it. I mentally stated that tomorrow I would again open to the energy and would like to be able to communicate with Ramsey in a more beneficial and traditional way. I felt there was a distinct purpose to what was happening to me. I knew I was not experiencing this for entertainment or curiosity. There was a reason for all that was happening and I wanted to be told, in a straightforward manner, what it was.

The next morning I prepared a tape recorder and placed it beside me. I sat down and began to meditate. I again called Ramsey to me and mentally requested to feel the energy. I restated my request to communicate with him. I wanted to know why he was here, what his intentions were and since he was my guide, what he could do for me.

I remember the energy again filling me. That wonderfully intense feeling of love and joy permeated my body. I felt a slight pressure in my throat area. I mentally asked, "Why are you here?" I felt my mouth open and words come out, but they weren't my words! I wasn't directing them, but they were answering my questions! With each word I felt a surge of energy flow through me and then recede. It was very jerky, as though the voice that flowed through me was clearing the way as it went. I continued to ask questions and receive answers. "I am here to teach," he said. "Where are you from?" I asked. "From the light, high light being," came the reply. I questioned further, "High light being?" I heard my voice reply, "Guide of high vibration, as you requested, will assist you with growth, here to teach." "Do you have a body?" I asked. Again, I heard my voice reply, "I am energy being. High guides do not have physical bodies. We have evolved to be one with the light. We teach other souls to also evolve higher. This is our purpose." The conversation went on, my mentally asking questions, and then hearing my voice reply with his words. As the communication went on, I noticed the voice getting smoother. Then I noticed I was also receiving mental images to go along with the voice. I would receive an image in my mind then words would follow to explain the image. At all times I felt totally in control. I felt only love coming from Ramsey. His words were chosen so perfectly. His message was love. His presence conveyed great wisdom, peace and love for me and for all of humanity. The presence I felt from Ramsey was incredible. I had never felt such unconditional love for everyone and every thing before. He was so caring and respectful of me, always letting me lead the way, always taking my "cues" as to how much I could understand at any one time. With each answer he gave I had three more questions to ask.

During that first week incredible things were happening to me physically. Each time I would sit down and relax, I would feel the energy fill me again. Each night I was awakened from my sleep to be filled with this energy. These times were very special to me as it felt as if I were being sent love from the higher realms. I was completely engulfed with the most peaceful and joyful contentment imaginable.

It was during this time my psychic abilities were revealing themselves. I was receiving mental images and whole chunks of data, which would tell a story. I was seeing past lives flash before me and along with them came concepts and understandings that were not verbalized. Someone would ask me a question and I would immediately receive the answer, or, I would wonder about something and suddenly receive an understanding of what I had questioned. At the time, I didn't understand where all this information was coming from, what it was called, or what I was to do with it. In looking back, I realize this intense energy flowing through me served to open my body's energy centers, opening me to access the Divine Source that is my soul.

I was very much in awe of what was happening to me. I felt something I had never felt and I knew it was much bigger than anything I could imagine. I realized that there was some wonderful guidance there for me and, although I could not understand why, this guidance wanted only to help me grow and learn. In light of this, I felt deeply honored and wished to express that I was thankful and I was willing to make a commitment. I spoke directly to the guide. I guess you would call it a prayer. I stated that I was willing to follow the instructions and guidance for whatever my purpose was to be. I wanted to show my commitment to this path and requested assistance in all areas to help me achieve whatever I was to do. I didn't know what my path was yet, but I wanted to help people and felt that somehow what was happening to me was the prelude to that.

As soon as I finished my "prayer," I heard the guide say I was not to pray to him. He said he is not to be viewed as a god. He is not to be viewed as superior to me, but as a master teacher. He said he is just a soul, the same as I am, the same as all souls. No one is any more a god than another. He has only evolved higher than I and through his own growth and evolution is able to guide and assist others. He explained that in helping others to grow, no matter what our level, we each evolve higher.

I was eager to share this new found guidance with family and friends. I called my friend, Wendy, who came right over. I explained what had happened, and she too wanted to experience it. I again accessed the energy and soon Wendy was also conversing with Ramsey. He told her of her guide and gave her some information on how she could access him herself. He explained that when we begin to "reach" (his word for souls that are searching for their purpose, for their own answers and truth) we attract a high-level guide—a guide who has evolved higher than the soul they are guiding. They are not to be confused with the guides that are around us on the astral plane. These guides, sometimes our deceased loved ones, are attached to us because of their love for us and usually have our best interests at heart. However, they are not usually any more evolved than we are and cannot serve the same purpose as the more highly evolved guides who wish to help in our spiritual growth. He explained that anyone who wishes to access this guidance can do so. All they need do is state their desire and intent and a guide will be there to assist them. It is the wish of all high-level guides that we come to know our true selves and that we evolve beyond what we perceive ourselves to be. They want us to understand what we truly are and that we are to become one with our higher selves, our soul. They want us to open our awareness and join them as one in the consciousness that we all share. It is their purpose to assist us in this endeavor, in any way we will permit.

When my husband, Clyde, came home I explained what had happened and he too began to converse with Ramsey. It seemed Ramsey had infinite patience for our questions. It was a good thing, because we were certainly trying hard to understand what was happening and continued to bombard him with questions regarding the universe, life, guides, God, etc. There were nights that we barely got any sleep, having stayed up until the wee hours being "taught" and learning more about all we asked. Soon the whole family was asking questions, my sons included. Ramsey had become part of the family. We were indeed learning a lot and we were very eager pupils.

During the next two weeks, I continued to access this source and even more amazing things started to happen. I would suddenly see pictures in my mind, pictures that were telling a story. Sometimes they were about a past life of mine or Clyde's. Sometimes, they were about what was currently going on with us. I would ask a question and wait for the pictures to begin. I would wonder about the whereabouts of an item and receive a mental picture telling me where it was. My children especially liked this, they found all sorts of things they had lost! However, there were some things they didn't appreciate about my pictures. Sometimes they would bicker between themselves as brothers will do, and would come to me for assistance, asking me to punish the one responsible for the latest dastardly deed. I would focus on a question and instantly *see* what had happened and I would *know* which child was telling the true story. I soon became known as the "lie detector." Obviously, there were no more secrets in our house!

Each day I felt more and more energy flowing through my body and each day I had access to more and more information, information about what people were thinking, about the other people in their lives, about how they felt and why they felt that way. I could see and understand many things, and it felt so effortless, so natural.

One evening, Clyde was asking Ramsey about his father, who had committed suicide by asphyxiating himself in his car when Clyde was only fourteen. He had asked Ramsey where his father was and why he had felt the need to end his life. Suddenly, I was filled with the most intense emotion I had ever felt. I began to see pictures in my mind of the car in which the death had occurred. Then it was as if I were him, reliving the experience, feeling all the emotions, expressing the sorrow and regret for leaving his children so soon. As tears streamed down my face and my body trembled, I mentally saw the scratching at the car door, then I felt the release at the moment of death. I mentally saw the car as if I were rising above it and then it was gone. As I composed myself, I heard his father's words in my mind. He expressed his feelings to the son he left so early. He told how he had been watching him and how he knows of his grandchildren. He spoke of his other children, of his life prior to his death and of his existence since. To say the least, we were stunned at this development.

I was also able to receive communication from those who had passed on!

There was a pattern emerging. Sometimes I would receive answers to my questions verbally, through my own voice, with no prior knowledge of what words were going to come out. This seemed to be the case when there was something of an intellectual nature that needed to be explained in detail. Sometimes I would receive mental images that would tell a story. This seemed to happen when I was accessing information about something such as a past life that required information about location, climate, terrain, housing, etc. Sometimes I would feel the response through my emotions. This happened when I accessed information about something of a personal nature, feelings, or circumstances. Sometimes I received all three, or a combination. I would receive the information in whatever form was easiest for me to understand. As I became more adept at this, I would request the information in whatever way I thought would be most helpful. I began to work with and develop these abilities. I requested assistance from the guides in using these new abilities for the highest good. It was important to me that they be used responsibly and only to help people.

This was a time of deep soul-searching for me—searching for answers to questions such as "Why me?" "Why now?" and "What am I to do with these abilities?" I was faced with many new feelings as I tried to integrate these abilities into my life. I found my logical mind balking at all that was happening. I went through stages when I would doubt if this was even happening at all. It did not fit into my logical world, or the world as I perceived it to be. Through all the doubts and insecurities, one thing was constant: the undeniable, total love and support I felt from Ramsey. He was there to address my fears, to help me understand what was happening and the reasons for it. He was there to help me understand the personal conflicts that kept arising as I continued to learn about myself. He answered my questions and provided new insights with the patience of a saint, never tiring of my self doubts or my curiosity, always helping me to the next level in my growth and understanding.

As I developed these new abilities, I began to share this wondrous thing with friends. I began to give them "readings." It was grand fun being able to access information they wanted and even grander being able to help them understand it. Not only would I receive information about their concerns, but I could access Ramsey who would explain to them why they were experiencing what they were experiencing and how this was helping them learn and grow and gave them insights as to how they might better handle the situation. It was truly amazing. He was unable to give anything but uplifting, empowering, truthful and loving guidance. It never ceased to amaze me that no matter what the question, no matter how depressing the answer I perceived, the words would always come in such a way as to empower and help the person. I loved helping people in this way.

As the days went by and I settled into my new role, I found that there were definite peaks and valleys. There were periods when I would delve into new information, striving to understand, asking questions, stretching my ideas and basically integrating the new information I was receiving. These times were followed by a period of "settling," in which I would need time to be alone, time to think, without trying to integrate any new ideas. I would spend this time enjoying my family, cooking, gardening, etc. After this settling period, I would again immerse myself in my new world, usually feeling the connection to the source as stronger than before. This pattern would repeat itself over and over. In questioning Ramsey about this, I was told that the conscious mind, the personality level, needs time to "catch up" with all it has been absorbing. I was undergoing many changes and this was my way of saying "slow down," I need a breather. As time went by however, I found these periods of settling were fewer and not as long in duration. I became more comfortable with the new person I was becoming, not needing to revert back to the way I had been.

As I continued to access this wealth of wisdom and knowledge that I perceived through my guide, Ramsey, I began to notice some subtle changes. My own spiritual growth was greatly accelerated as I accessed his words for insights on how to deal with everyday situations and for new and higher perspectives on the way I viewed the world. I needed to replace my old perceptions with higher, more loving points of view. I wanted to understand the world, to really understand how I could view the chaos around me and not feel depressed. I had always felt powerless when I would see pain and suffering, feeling great pain and sorrow for those people I viewed as victims. Through Ramsey's guidance, I was able to understand that there are reasons for everything that is occurring, and once I understood this from the broader perspective, rather than from my limited earthly perceptions, I felt very empowered. I could see there really was good in all situations. The most growth comes out of what we view as the worst of times. I understood all that had taken place over the course of history was a catalyst for change and can be understood very differently from the soul level.

CHAPTER 5

Integration

THE TIME I TOOK TO ACCESS THIS connection was reducing itself. From the half hour it took at the beginning, it soon was down to fifteen minutes, then ten, then one, then thirty seconds, then it seemed as though Ramsey was with me all the time. I would feel the energy within me at all times, rather than it filling me when I focused on it and consciously brought it to myself. I was able to access the wisdom and love on a continual basis, bringing through the information and direction I needed without any prior forethought. When I didn't speak out loud, I would hear the voice in my mind, as responses to my own thoughts. The voice was always uplifting, loving, and directed toward my spiritual growth, assisting me to learn about myself and to see the world in new ways. I was indeed learning much from this guide.

About this time, I noticed that, at times when Ramsey would speak, my own voice would begin to come through intermittently. It was hard to tell which was which. When I accessed the guidance of Ramsey, it felt like myself answering. Gone was the feeling of switching back and forth. I wondered about this and one day I questioned him about it. I was told that through my growth, I had been able to raise my vibration to the level necessary to connect directly to the "Whole." I no longer needed a guide to bridge the gap and I was now able to tap into the universal source on my own. My mind immediately doubted that this was possible and I felt that familiar self-doubt creep back in.

It just so happened that the following weekend I attended the San Francisco Whole Life Expo, an exposition of every conceivable kind of New Age and holistic practitioner, demonstrations, speakers and products. As I browsed down aisle after aisle, taking in all the excitement, I passed an author who was promoting her book without taking an interest in what she was saying. I was two booths past her when the familiar voice in my head instructed me to "go back." It said I needed to hear what she had to say. Having learned to listen to this voice, I proceeded back to speak to her. Her name is Susan Shumsky and she was promoting her book, *Divine Revelation* (Simon and Schuster, 1996). I found out she was scheduled to give a lecture that afternoon, which I attended. During her lecture, she talked about our "direct connection to the Divine." She explained that many people who channel are not even aware that they are actually "speaking through" from the Divine Source. They give credit to other entities because they do not realize that we all are capable of accessing Divine guidance for ourselves. This was the message I was to hear.

I realized a shift had taken place in my perception (my idea of what is possible). From that time on, I did not communicate with a specific guide such as Ramsey. I was able to ask for guidance and receive answers from the universal source. Once we are able to break through the veil of illusion of our conscious minds and our personality and ego levels, we can access the whole to which we are all a part. We no longer need to view everything as something outside of ourselves. Ramsey had led me to understand and accept that this connection I was experiencing was a connection to the Divine Source of all knowledge. It is a natural part of my soul's evolution and is available to all of us. I no longer had a need to hold onto the perception of a guide as separate from myself.

The universal source, which some refer to as the Consciousness, God and various other names, is the essence of what we all are at the soul level. We all have the ability, and more than that, we have the destiny to connect with this universal source. The evolution of our species depends on this connection. Once we are aware of the Divine Source that links us all, once we really understand to what extent we are connected to each other, the world will indeed undergo some major changes. To see others, to see world events, to see situations as I do, using this connection, is to indeed live in a wonderful place. To bring this insight, love, and wisdom through to our daily lives on a regular, ongoing basis will transform every part of our beings. Once we are able to rise above and transcend the personality level and the limiting and hurtful perceptions we hold about ourselves and others and we realize what and who we truly are, there will be nothing on this planet that will not be profoundly affected by it. Within us all lies a soul waiting to make the connection to its origin, to the whole. Your soul is waiting to bring its wisdom through to your daily life so you can begin to evolve as you were meant to.

When my Kundalini activated, the only reference I had was that I had accessed a spirit guide. This was the way in which my soul needed to connect. I needed this guidance to assist me with each step along the way. This was necessary for me to overcome my self-doubt, shyness and insecurity. My soul had provided what it needed to allow for the connection to happen, through this filter of my current lifetime. Given the same circumstances, another may perceive these experiences differently. They may describe "talking to God" or "being filled with the Holy Spirit," or any number of explanations that would enable them to experience and integrate what was happening. We all interpret and express things differently. There is not any one way that is "right." All is created and experienced as we ourselves direct. The self will always draw to itself what it needs to grow. The vehicle is unimportant. Only the arrival matters to your soul.

Part II

Understanding

It is one of the commonest of mistakes to consider that the limit of our power of perception is also the limit of all there is to perceive.
—C. W. Leadbeater

CHAPTER 6

Psychic Abilities

I T IS IMPORTANT TO UNDERSTAND the function psychic abilities play in our spiritual growth. The onset of these abilities is a natural progression of our expanding perceptions and awareness. As our bodies and minds become more aligned with the Divine Source, it is perfectly natural, even expected, to be able to feel and comprehend the feelings and experiences of the other parts of our Self. The existence of psychic abilities does not, however, guarantee a high level of spiritual awareness and you must use discernment when receiving intuitive guidance from others. Always listen to your inner guidance, follow only what rings of truth to you. Accept only what feels right. If you are receiving true guidance, accessed from the Divine Source, you will *feel* the truth in it. You will feel uplifted, loved and empowered and you will have a deeper understanding of yourself, enabling you to progress further along your spiritual path.

Through this process and as a result of the Kundalini activation, I have received many psychic abilities. I am now clairvoyant (able to see images), clairaudient (able to hear from the spirit world) and clairsentient (able to feel communications through my body). I can see and hear those spirits who have passed on to the other side, relaying messages from them to their loved ones who remain on the earth plane. I can tune into people and feel as they do, understanding their fears, difficulties and potential. I can see and interpret past lives and future probabilities and access guidance to explain the connection between these things and the soul I am reading for. Distance seems to make no difference, nor does it matter if I know the person or not. I find I am able to read animals as well, and can interpret how they feel at any given moment.

I would like to share some experiences from my early intuitive readings because these experiences opened my eyes to the continuity of all life. As I taught, I learned, realizing we are all here to help each other expand and grow. I never focused on these abilities as an end or means in and of themselves. They have always taken a back seat to my continuing drive to merge into full consciousness with the Divine Source.

These early experiences served to broaden my understanding of what my abilities were and what I could do with them. As I began to use these gifts to assist people, I realized it was very important to me to use them responsibly. For this reason, I am selective with my readings. I shy away from those who want someone to tell them if they are going to win the lottery, or marry a rich man. Instead, I focus on providing guidance to those who truly want to grow spiritually, people who are trying to understand themselves and their lives. I provide them with answers and insights to understand their circumstances and those around them. I give them the confidence and assurance they need to proceed to their next level and show them where to look to improve the quality of their lives and increase their happiness. I give them the information their soul would give them, had they their own connection.

An interesting distinction I have found is that I cannot read the physical things. For example, if I view two souls and it appears to me clairvoyantly that they love each other, I am unable to tell if they are husband and wife or boyfriend and girlfriend. Because I read the soul level, the physical legality of the marriage does not come to me, only the way they feel about each other. Likewise, if two people are married, I am able to tell if they are loving, distant or fighting with each other. When I speak of closeness or distance, I am referring to emotional closeness, rather than physical closeness or distance. Sometimes we are physically close to people, but feel isolated from them. Similarly, there are those who live across the country, but we maintain a deep connection and closeness. For example, I once read for a woman who asked about her brother. I felt he was cut off from the rest of the family and the father had washed his hands of him. I did not know the specific circumstances, or what this meant physically, until she informed me her brother was incarcerated and was serving a lengthy prison sentence. The emotions I felt were from the soul level, but I was unable to see the physical circumstances.

These physical things do not exist on the soul level and the constant factor in all my readings is how one feels. It is their perceptions (thoughts) that dictate their circumstances and experiences. It is the experiences that are recorded in the energy field. I have come to understand the only things that truly matter are those things that exist on the soul level. Everything else is just window dressing, the trappings we have created for the expression of what we feel within our souls.

On another occasion, I received information about a client who was scheduled to come in later in the day, from her father who had transitioned[6] several years earlier! I was expecting Rose at noon, but about 9:00 A.M. I started receiving messages from a spirit who said he was her father and he was worried about her boyfriend. I was a little unsure about this and not quite convinced I was actually hearing what I thought. I was understandably nervous about relaying this message to her. When she arrived, her father was present in the room. When I say he was present, what I mean is, I was able to see his spirit clairvoyantly. He was trying to give me messages to relay to her. When the session began, I asked about her family members and asked if her father had passed away. She said he had, about six years earlier. She went on to say she had come to ask about her boyfriend! I was amazed at what had occurred and a little relieved to find out I was not imagining what I had heard. I told her about his earlier visit to me and about his being present in the room. At first, she was not sure if this spirit was her natural father or her stepfather, whom she also considered to be her father. I asked this spirit for clarification and he showed me a tattoo on his upper arm. Rose confirmed that her natural father had a tattoo on his arm, the same as I had described. He went on to say he had been watching her in her kitchen and often placed himself near the corner window. When I relayed this message, Rose gasped in surprise and confided to me she has repeatedly seen something in that corner and hasn't been able to figure out what. I felt very honored to be able to accommodate this communication between Rose and her father.

During another reading, I was able to provide a message to assist a woman who was grieving over the loss of her son, who had transitioned a year before. Marsha called asking if I could do a reading on her son, Bruce. She said he had died under mysterious circumstances; that is, she felt the truth about his death had been kept from her by his wife and she had been searching for a way to contact him. I could sense she was in a lot of pain over this and I had her come right over. I explained that I couldn't promise I would be able to contact Bruce, or that he would want to speak to me, but I would try. I asked her not to tell me anything about his death, as I didn't want to take the chance that the information I received would be colored by what she told me. I always prefer to read someone that I have no prior knowledge of, because I feel I am able to more accurately convey the information and the client also has the comfort that the communication is genuine. When we began the session, I felt the presence of Bruce very strongly. He knew she was desperately trying to contact him and he also wanted to communicate with her. As I focused on him, I felt my chest become very heavy and felt an intense pressure throughout my chest area. Then the room began to spin and I felt disorientation and an inability to focus my eyes or mind. What I was experiencing was delirium. I conveyed this to

Marsha, still unsure of the cause of his death. She told me he died at home of pneumonia, which would explain the chest pain and the delirium from his high fever. He perceived his death as being caused from this sickness and he placed no blame on his wife. In fact, he expressed great concern for the pain she was feeling since his death. This made Marsha feel better, though she was still having a hard time getting on with her life. Bruce then gave me a vision of a tiny picture of him and said his mother holds it in her hand and thinks about him. Marsha instinctively grabbed for her necklace, a locket that has a picture of Bruce inside. She said she holds it while she talks to him. He went on to say he wanted her to quit grieving for him and pay more attention to his little brother who really needs her. Marsha then told me she has a younger son who is developmentally slow. The two boys were really close and Bruce tended to watch over his younger brother. Marsha felt somewhat relieved in having communicated with Bruce, but she was still worried about something that had happened before he transitioned. She went on to say she had told him a lie before he died, but before she could finish, Bruce told me to assure her he knew she had lied and it was OK. He then conveyed that he "already knew" and there was no need for her to feel bad about it. She never told me what the lie was, but she seemed to be relieved at hearing this and said his response made perfect sense to her. Not all messages I receive from spirit are as clear as Bruce's. There was obviously great love between mother and son to allow for such a communication.

It is always amazing to me to find that our loved ones remain around us after they transition. They are aware of our thoughts and actions. I have had spirits communicate to me what they thought about their funerals, usually expressing concern for the loved ones who are in pain. It must be very frustrating to witness those you left behind in such pain and be unable to communicate with them to ease their suffering. I had a session with a young woman named Lisa who had lost her father two years earlier. She felt she had not told him how much she loved him and was missing him terribly. When I focused on her father's soul, I received a lot of information from him. He told me that he watches his granddaughter, especially when she "sits on the floor by the ruffles." He then commented on how much he liked the picture they had made. Lisa, excited in receiving communication from her father, explained that her daughter sits on the floor, next to her bed, which is covered in ruffles, every day as she watches TV. She then told me of a picture of her father, that was taken from a brochure made by his previous employer. They had the picture blown up into a large photo for display at the funeral, and later displayed it in the hallway of her mother's home.

As I read people, I find they usually already know what I tell them. Since I read them at the soul level, my interpretation usually confirms what they already knew deep down. However, since we don't always act the way we feel, it can be very helpful to know what feelings exist at the soul level of those around us. For instance, because of her children, one client was feeling guilty about a divorce. She was worried they would resent her or feel deprived not having their father around. As I focused on them, I was able to describe each child's personality traits and emotional qualities and let her know how they felt about her and their father. This alleviated her fears, knowing they felt secure and loved.

Something else I have noticed while doing readings is that whenever there is a health problem, from either a person who transitioned, or someone still living on the earth plane, I can easily see the affected area. When Lisa first told me her father had passed, I saw a problem in his head. It seemed like something internal and she confirmed he had a stroke, which was the cause of his death. A very common illness I see is lung cancer. Even if the person does not have cancer, but they are a smoker, I immediately see a darkness in their lungs. One client was describing her boyfriend who had chased someone over a fence. I saw he had fallen on his shoulder and injured it and it still caused him pain. She confirmed he has had two surgeries on the shoulder since the fall. When I focus on a soul, either living here, or who has transitioned, the first thing I usually see is any illness in the body. Sometimes, I feel the sensation of the illness in my own body, although I have never felt pain. Other times, I see the affected area of the body. This is not a diagnosis by any means, I am only able to determine the affected area and feel if this is an injury or a cause of death. When the body experiences an injury or illness, it is held in our body's energy field. By following the illness back to the source, it is possible to identify what triggered the illness or what attitude or perception contributed to that person's propensity to manifest the illness to begin with.

From time to time, I have used my abilities to assist clients with health issues. The first time I discovered that I could be effective in this way was during an intuitive session with a woman who has since become a dear friend. Susan had come to ask about her dog, Max. He was a German shepherd that Susan had been showing for some time. She had to withdraw him from the show circuit due to recurring seizures. She had been working with her veterinarian and also using various holistic remedies, but to no avail. Max had been placed on seizure medication but the seizures continued. There was no apparent trigger for the seizures and when they happened, Susan was terrified. Max was so big she was unable to hold him still when a seizure occurred and she feared for his safety. The first time I met Susan I was struck by the incredible gift she has with her dogs, such a connection and love flowed between them. This is what brought Susan to me to begin with, her incredible love for Max. As I focused on Max, I was amazed at the clearness I felt from him. (I have found that animals are very easy to read because they are so honest, much like little children in their innocence and openness.) I asked him about the seizures and I felt a pulling sensation in the back of my neck and then the motion of being pulled backwards, by the nape of the neck, totally helpless to stop it. I realized I was feeling what Max did when he had a seizure. I conveyed this to Susan and she confirmed that during a seizure, he is pulled backwards as I described, almost as if he is going to flip over. I kept asking what was causing the seizures but I was unable to intuit anything more. I had a feeling that I could help Max and so I took Susan's phone number and address in case I was able to access more information.

The next day I was thinking about Max and wondered if I had not asked the right questions. I had asked, "What caused the seizures?" Perhaps, he was unable to tell me because he didn't know. I felt I needed to see him again and called Susan. She had me come right over. This time when I focused on Max I asked him what he felt like just *before* the seizures. I got the impression that he knew exactly what I meant and I began to feel what he did. I could tell that he knew they were coming because there was always a sharp pointed pain on his upper back, followed seconds later by the seizure. The pain triggered something that ran up his spine into the base of his skull. He was aware that when he felt this pain, the seizure was coming and it terrified him. He would brace himself for it and felt terrible because he had no control over it. Afterward, he felt as if he had done something bad because Susan was afraid and he didn't understand why or make the connection. Once I felt the spot in my own body where Max's pain occurred, I pointed to it on him. I ran my hand over his back and further focused on this area. Immediately my spine twisted, throwing me to one side. I realized his back was out of alignment!

I conveyed this revelation to Susan and the next week she was able to get Max in to see a chiropractor who works on animals. The X-ray confirmed there were several vertebrae out of alignment, in the exact spot I had pointed to! Her vet told her this was very unusual, not something they would ever look for as a cause for seizures, but that it had obviously been the cause of Max's seizures. His back was put back in alignment and the seizures stopped. Several months later, the seizures began again and a quick focus on Max told me his back was out of alignment again. Once it was corrected, the seizures stopped again.

This experience taught me a lot. I never presume anything during a reading. If I don't get information one way, I rephrase the question. Sometimes, a different angle is all that is required. The information is always there to be tapped into, it is just a matter of learning how to retrieve and interpret it.

As I became more and more used to these abilities, I wanted to understand how I was obtaining the information, I needed to know how "it" worked. I tapped into the universal source and received an explanation of the process: We are all one soul, one consciousness, sometimes referred to as the Whole. We are energy vibrations, expressions of the whole, manifesting ourselves in the physicality. Each one of us affects the energy around us by our thoughts and this, subsequently, affects others. No thought is private. When you have a thought, you are creating. The thought takes form and therefore, comes into existence. It then exists in the collective consciousness and ultimately becomes a mass-thought form. The world we all experience is a direct result of all thoughts that have ever existed. It is an outward manifestation of our collective thoughts. We have collectively created our reality. When I read for someone, I tap into the energy surrounding them, the energy created by their thoughts, and clairvoyantly see the information. If they ask about a distant family member or friend, they are tuning into that person's energy vibration with their thought. I am then able to read the family member by tapping into that stream of energy. All souls exist at one soul level, tied together by the energy, forming the collective consciousness. Since the consciousness that exists at the soul level is not limited by physicality (there is no time or space beyond this physical plane), I am able to access the same information regardless of distance or the form of communication used (i.e. in person, telephone or computer).

These abilities I have, these gifts that I received as a result of the Kundalini activation, are actually the norm. We all have this sixth sense, or as some call it, intuition. It is more developed in some than others. The plan for our species was not to live in darkness, cut off from each other and the other realms, but to have these abilities to use in our daily lives. We will discuss this "sixth sense" at length in Chapter 11.

Past Lives, Present Realities

THE ISSUE OF PAST LIVES IS A CONTROVERSIAL ONE. Although the reality of reincarnation is accepted by many religions throughout the world, in our own country there are many who still doubt its existence. I counted myself among them until I directly experienced several of my own past lives and relived countless others for my clients. After experiencing the connections between these past experiences that are embedded in our energy fields and our current lifetimes, I know that we've all had many lives. In this chapter, I will share some of my experiences from past-life readings. As you read through them, think about your own life, your own sensitive issues, unexplainable fears and recurring patterns and ask yourself if they could be rooted in one of your past lives.

One of my first readings was with a quiet woman named Carol. Carol had questions about her children and husband. She also asked about her past lives. I immediately saw two lives and began to describe them to her. Each one was a situation very much like the one she is currently in, a family circumstance that involved her caring for those around her, with no regard for herself. She had lived selfless lives and was repeating the pattern. Not surprisingly, the issues she was dealing with during her current life had to do with standing up for herself, putting herself first and attending to her own needs. As I recounted the most recent past life for her, I saw her as a young boy on a boat. As my clairsentient abilities took over, I felt myself engulfed in darkness and was sinking lower and lower. I felt I could not get air and then felt fish swarming all around me. They swarmed and engulfed me so totally, all I could do was wave my hands frantically in an attempt to fling them away. I did not feel pain, just the emotions of the situation. I was being smothered by them and my whole body was jerking and seemed to spasm while I continued flinging my arms, trying to keep the fish away from me. I felt a release and peace flowed over me. I realized Carol had died in this way during that lifetime. I opened my eyes to see Carol with tears streaming down her face. She said what she had just witnessed was exactly what she has felt like on numerous occasions throughout her life: the smothering feeling, the frantic flinging to keep her face clear and the hatred of fish. She went on to tell me that she had no idea why all her life she had such an aversion to fish. She had been raised in the Midwest, far from any body of water, yet she loathed fish in any form. She was unable to eat them and felt uncomfortable even viewing them in an aquarium. Swimming or boating was out of the question. As she watched me "live out" her previous death experience, she saw these things she had wondered about during her life come to the surface and she now understood the reasons for them. It was at that moment I understood the value of past-life regression and how this information can help someone in understanding their current life experience.

Many times, we carry things with us from a past life: fears or phobias of unknown origin, the mysterious illness that modern medicine is unable to pinpoint, the strong reaction to meeting a new person or the feeling of deja vu experienced by so many people. These are all examples of experiences that can hold their roots within your soul's memory, encoded throughout your body's DNA, serving as reminders and catalysts to further our evolution. There is a genetic road map within each of us. It contains the identities we have held during our past lives. During our current life, "triggers" will sound. These are the soul's way of bringing these past lives to the surface. When we explore ourselves further, the "triggers" we have experienced during our current lives will be brought to the forefront, asking to be understood and integrated, bringing us one step further in the evolution of our soul. Not all past lives affect the current one. Each life carries its own message, each building on the next.

A woman I know, who has a recurring problem with her lower legs and feet, is a classic example. It is hard for her to get around due to the pain in her legs. She has had several surgeries, but nothing seems to alleviate the problem. She has created her life to be in a state of constant motion. She never has enough time, is always in a hurry and can't seem to go fast enough. She is at a loss to understand why she is this way. It seems normal to her and is the way she has always been. Her health is suffering as a result. When I did a reading on her, I saw a previous life as a distance runner. I saw her running footraces, across very rugged terrain. She had been quite famous and derived great importance and self-worth from her running. This is an obvious scenario and it is not hard to understand that she has carried the racing mentality into this lifetime. The perpetual problems with her legs and feet are reminiscent of a distance runner, and are her soul's way of acting out her previous lifetime in an attempt to capture her attention. Unknowingly, she had tied her self-worth in this lifetime to that which provided it in her past life.

My husband, Clyde, had been experiencing his own "trigger" for many years before I accessed my clairvoyant abilities and we were able to make the connection. Clyde has always been an athletic, sports-minded, active person and routinely participated in organized softball and basketball leagues. Twenty-one years ago he joined a different softball team than he had previously played with. On that team, he met Stan, and felt an immediate rapport with him. They were instantly comfortable with each other and have remained close through the years, despite Clyde's move to a different part of the state. It was during the time Clyde joined Stan's softball team that he began to have pain in his right shoulder. The pain was excruciating and at times he was unable to lift the arm above his shoulder level. The condition would worsen at times and lessen at other times, but it has been persistent throughout the past twenty-one years. Clyde consulted several doctors, many X-rays were taken, yet there has never been a concrete diagnosis. They usually referred to it as a "muscle thing" and antiinflammatory drugs were prescribed. He chalked it up as "one of those things you have to live with" and dealt with it as best he could.

During one of the sessions in which I read Clyde's past lives for him, I saw a lifetime he had previously had with Stan. I saw they had been soldiers in the Scottish Revolution. As Clyde listened, I recounted his death experience from that lifetime. I saw before me the battlefield, English soldiers on horseback and Scotsmen on foot. I saw the bodies as they lay, the blood covering the ground and I felt the violence in the air. A scene played out in my mind's eye of Clyde and Stan rushing forward, seemingly oblivious to the insurmountable odds of the situation. I saw a mounted English soldier come straight at Clyde, running him over with his horse, pushing him to the ground. As he fell, the scene played in slow motion. I saw the detail of the fall. I saw him fall on his right side, directly on the right shoulder and the horse running over him, trampling his head and shoulders. Stan threw himself on top of Clyde, trying to revive him. As he was bent over Clyde, he was struck in the back and collapsed on top of him. They died together in this way, brothers to the end.

When I had finished the reading and regained my composure, Clyde and I looked at each other in amazement. It was then that he realized his shoulder pain first began at the time in his life when he met Stan. The recognition that Clyde's soul felt for Stan triggered the physical response most closely related to the lifetime they previously shared and it was again manifesting itself. After this revelation became known to Clyde, his shoulder pain began to get better and within a month of understanding this connection, this pain he had lived with for twenty-one years was gone. Three years have passed and it has not recurred.

After my initial opening and during that two-week period afterwards, I was experiencing many episodes of my own past lives being played out in my mind. This is characteristic of the Kundalini energy, bringing past experiences through to the conscious mind to be integrated. As if I were watching a movie screen, I witnessed and experienced many of the lives I have had. I felt the emotions surrounding them and understood how they are affecting me in this lifetime. Each memory seemed to be another piece to the puzzle. I saw my most previous lifetime in which I had been killed during World War II. This helped me to understand my lifelong abhorrence to war. I am not talking about a healthy dislike of violence, but a strong emotional and physical reaction that I've experienced all my life. As a little girl, when my parents would watch movies or TV shows depicting war, I would feel sick to my stomach, be unable to sleep and would retain a feeling of uneasiness for three or four days after such a viewing. It was as if I could actually feel the pain I saw. I would feel the emotions that come along with experiencing war first hand. The anguish, the death, the fear, the confusion and hopelessness would become part of me as I saw these scenes. Not surprisingly, I avoided anything that reminded me of war in an attempt to avoid having such upsetting reactions.

The ocean has always been a source of fear for me. As a child, I never visited the ocean and did not know why I feared it so much. I am a good swimmer, and water has never been a problem for me. One morning shortly after my initial "opening," I was awakened by a vivid dream in which I was small child. I physically felt as if I could not breath and this brought me out of my dream. However, the "dream" continued after I woke and I began to see and feel water washing over me. I looked up and saw the surface of the water, perhaps a foot above my head and felt the waves carrying me forward and back. I was aware that I was very close to shore and I had an understanding that I was in the ocean. I felt something hitting me, washing over me, something that was in the water, but I didn't know what. I was physically feeling the sensations and seeing what I saw as that small child. I was reliving my death from a previous life. As this memory flooded through my mind, it brought with it the knowledge of that lifetime. I had been drowned off the island of Crete, I was approximately two years old. I then saw my mother crying at the shoreline, crying for her baby. She was comforted by a man. This man was her husband, but he was not my father. I can't explain how I knew that—the information just appeared in my awareness as the memory flooded in. The woman I saw as my mother is the same soul that is my son, Zachary, in this lifetime. The man who was her husband is the soul that was my father in this lifetime. This explains the great bond and connection my father and Zachary always shared.

This is a common scenario. Often, souls reincarnate into the same family group from previous lifetimes. Love is the strongest bond and it transcends all time and dimensions. A soul will often take a different gender or relationship than they previously had. For instance, you may have been married to someone in a past life and reincarnate as their child or sibling. These groupings of souls who seem to follow each other from lifetime to lifetime are referred to as "soul groups." Each one of us has many soul groups, sometimes overlapping, sometimes not. Some souls in the group may choose not to reincarnate and remain in the spirit dimensions to continue their growth and assist others in their group as a guide or teacher. In a more general way, all the souls on earth are one soul group, interconnected to one another and in agreement to evolve through the physicality of the common experience they share.

Many times people feel as though they have had a past life with someone in their current life. I get many such questions. It is interesting to note that as I focus on these relation-ships and relay the information I receive, many people shout out in recognition, saying they "knew it." We all have these intuitive feelings, yet we are unable to trust them or under-stand what they are.

When someone asks about a past life, I don't receive knowledge about all their past lives. Rather, I receive only the information about one, two, or occasionally, three lives that are affecting the current lifetime. Sometimes, it has to do with a situation or circumstance they have faced in a prior life and are again dealing with. Sometimes, the information that comes through and connects to the current life has to do with a cur-rent relative or friend who shared a prior life and may be here to assist in their spiritual growth. Often times, there is a pat-tern that is being repeated and the soul is trying to get their attention so the lesson may be learned, the cycle broken and the needed growth, experienced. Always, upon hearing a past life described, an inner connection is made, and there is a recognition or trigger within the person. As the pieces fall into place, they gain a deeper understanding of themselves and their journey. As with everything on our spiritual path, we are shown what we can accept and integrate, for our highest good, at any given time along our journey.

C H A P T E R 8

God

JUST WHERE DOES OUR DIVINE GUIDANCE come from? That depends on your perception of God. Your perceptions are every thing. They are the reason you experience fear, faith, joy, and sorrow. They are the reason you are a Divine being with the ability to create and experience with just a thought. There are so many faces God wears, so many names we use to describe this unseen force and so many different ways to show our devotion. The way in which you have chosen to perceive God will determine the experience you will have as you open to receive Divine guidance. It is your perceptions that will allow or disallow the experience.

Some perceptions allow for an opening to and direct experience of the Divine Source and some will not. Those who view themselves as separate from God will create that experience. In fact, that is what we have been doing throughout our incarnations, having the experience of being separate from God. But those who recognize God in all forms will be open to experience the Divine directly. Sometimes, it is our own fears that keep us from what we want most. Those who have a rigid belief and preconceived expectation of what God is have closed themselves off from experiencing directly the infinite essence of God. No matter what form God takes in their lives, they won't recognize it if they believe God only looks and acts a certain way.

Everything man-made must be stripped away if you are to open to experience the larger part of yourself. The trappings, superstitions and dogmas of religion, the fears and beliefs that have been handed down to us must be released in order to accept that which cannot be named. Once you open yourself fully to the universe, without any preconceived ideas, you will be transformed by what you find. You will then understand that any attempt to contain or label the source of divinity only limits your understanding and experience of it.

As you open honestly, free from religion and fear, you become as a small child. In this innocence, there is only love. From these eyes, you can finally see what is apparent and you will no longer need the vehicle of religion as a source to bring God to you. I believe it was easier for me to accept what has happened to me because I didn't have deeply rooted religious beliefs in this lifetime. For this I am thankful. I was not hindered by fear of the unknown, fear of "evil" or fear that I was experiencing something that was "other than God." I was therefore free to experience the wonder of this natural transformation innocently, as it is meant to be.

In opening to Divine guidance, you will be led to expand your perception of yourself. Where you now perceive yourself as an individual, separate from everything, you will be led to expand and mature that perception to allow for a continuing experience of unity with everything. The perception of individuality is replaced with the perception of peace and connection to all of creation. I will share an analogy with you that was shown to me to help me understand this connection: Imagine a glass of water. Within the glass there are individual molecules of water. However, when the individuals are all together, they make up the whole—the glass of water. We are like these molecules. We are each individuals, yet, at the soul level, at the source, we are all one. The glass of water represents the consciousness of the whole. If we were those molecules, we could say we are aware that we are an individual molecule, and perhaps we would say that we also see those molecules around us and know that they too are individuals. But, we would be unable to see the rest of the glass, we would not be aware of the whole that we were all contributing to. Once we open our awareness to see beyond our own individuality and that of those immediately around us, we would discover that we are but one aspect of the whole consciousness. It is the purpose of the soul's incarnations to connect with this consciousness. It is the wish of our soul that we draw from that whole, that glass of water, at all times. This is what is referred to as "being your higher-self" or for Christians, "Christ Consciousness." This connection is possible for all of us. Once the connection is made, once your conscious mind understands the connection and becomes open to guidance from your soul, you will be catapulted toward that goal. You will find many things being presented to you, books, lectures or chance meetings. Your soul will work overtime to see that you are able to achieve and maintain that connection. This is the evolution of our species, to tap into the Whole, to connect with the Source and to live our lives from that place of higher guidance and understanding.

The frequency of love illuminates the soul. When you open yourself purely and honestly, with only love in your heart, you will be creating the vibration of energy that draws the experience of God to you. This Divine energy is the light within you. It is your own divinity and allows you to experience a part of yourself that exists beyond your physical body and beyond your current conscious perceptions. It is simply a leap of faith. You need only drop your safety net and jump.

Through my experiences since the Kundalini awakened, I have had to examine my own ideas about God. There certainly was a higher power flowing through my body. I was unable to find a reference for what I was experiencing in the religions of the world. Yet, it was obvious, as my body literally shook in vibration and my awareness perceived previously unknown insights, that this power was within me. It is a part of me, as it is of you. It is not something separate or outside of us that we are to approach. Rather, it is a source within us that we can awaken to perceive when we are ready to reconnect and end our soul's experience of separation.

As I searched to understand, I was led to the teachings of the Essenes[7]. These profound people had existed during one of the most turbulent times in our history, yet they remained centered in the source of Divine creation, passing on the teachings that would influence many visionaries and healers such as Elijah, John the Baptist and the Master Teacher, Jesus.

The Essenes believed in a universal Law that governs all that takes place in the universe and all other universes. The Law is the greatest and only power in the universe and all other laws and things are a part of the one Law. This universal Law has been symbolized by the Essenes as a tree, called the Tree of Life. This teaching was symbolized in their Tree of Life, which depicts man as a unit of energy, thoughts and emotions and a life force constantly communing with the totality of energies in the universe. They believed that deviations from the universal Law were the cause of illness and disharmony and that it is these deviations that take one farther from the experience of God within themselves. They believed that the sum total of life on all planets in the universe was part of a larger whole, contributing to a cosmic ocean of thought, or cosmic consciousness. The symbolic Tree of Life enabled the Essenes to understand how they were surrounded by the forces, or angels, from the visible world of nature and the invisible cosmic world. They held daily communions to show how each of these forces is utilized in man's body and the consciousness.

The Sevenfold Peace of the Essenes was the summation of their inner teaching. Their Tree of Life and the communions taught man his relationship with the forces of the visible and invisible worlds. The Sevenfold Peace explains man's relationship to the parts of his own being and to his fellow man, showing how to create peace and harmony in the seven categories of life: physical, mental, emotional, social, cultural, the relationship with nature and the relationship to the entire cosmos. (It is interesting to note that these seven categories correlate to the lessons of the seven main chakras.)

Through these teachings, I found the basis for all I was experiencing. What really struck me was that the Essene teachings were not a religion, nor were they an abstract idea to aspire to. They were a way of life, so much a part of their being that there could be no separation from their lives and their spirituality. These teachings were not something that one read from a book or were told about, they were something that was lived every day. For the Essenes, God was realized, understood and experienced in the daily observance of the world around them, in nature, in each other and in themselves. These teachings struck me at the depth of my soul. They shouted to me that this is the way it was meant to be, before mankind created so much confusion and deception, before we evolved so far from our center and were unable to see.

These simple truths that are apparent to those whose eyes are open to see require nothing more than direct observation and open contemplation. These teachings helped me shed the last vestiges of being raised in a Christian society. They allowed me to surrender my mind entirely to the nameless source of my being. When this shift occurred, I experienced an immediate deepening of the Divine connection flowing through me. I began to meditate for longer periods, wanting only to merge with the Divine Source more fully. It was shortly after that (one year and eight months after the initial Kundalini awakened) that the Kundalini continued its ascent, through my lower three chakras, merging them into one cohesive unit. (See Appendix A for an explanation of this process.) I was able to clairvoyantly see this process as it happened and once the Divine energy had seated itself in my heart chakra, I experienced a dramatic shift in my perceptions and reality.

In the process of opening to experience your Divine Source, and because of what we have been taught regarding what God is, you may need to perceive something outside of you is leading you. That is the reason my perceptions allowed for the experiencing of my guide, Ramsey, and later for the internal guidance of Jesus. As I was led along, I was urged to abandon these perceptions and embrace what I was being led to: the realization that we are all Divine beings, able to experience that divinity directly; expand our perceptions past individuality; draw directly from the Divine Source for knowledge and the continued evolution of our soul.

Open your heart as you reach for Divine guidance. Do not let your mind hinder you with logic and rationale. Drop your perceptions and become as a small child. Jesus said, *The works that I do shall you do also; and greater works than these shall you do* (John 14:12). Call on whatever guidance you need to bring you to that realization. When you tap into that Divine spark, merge with it. You will derive clarity, love, joy and creative expression beyond what you ever dreamed possible.

CHAPTER 9

Catalysts for Change

THERE IS A PHOTOGRAPH I HAVE TUCKED AWAY in a box, a photograph that I can't bear to display, yet one that I can't seem to throw away. The photo is of a little girl, about seven years of age. Her clothes are dirty and obviously a size or two too small. Her hair is dirty and matted. Her teeth are yellow from neglect. She bows her head, too shy and insecure to look up at the camera. In looking at this photo, I can feel her emotions. I feel her insecurity. I feel her need for approval, for attention and for acceptance. I feel her trying to reach out to others, yet feeling too insecure to take the chance. The other kids make fun of her, torment her for the way she looks, for her lack of social skills. She feels so alone, so isolated. She feels so different from the rest.

I see that deep inside she holds secrets. She hides the mother who, tied up in her own turmoil, was unable to express love, was unable to provide the basics of physical cleanliness or home-cooked meals. The mother who did not show an interest in the girl. The mother who did not allow her to play with friends, making it hard to keep the few she was able to make. The mother who could not provide a foundation the girl could feel secure in. The mother who could not provide encouragement to her daughter. I also see the father, a man who loved the girl, but in his own attempt to distance himself from the mother, was unable to be close enough to provide what she needed. Then, there is the best kept secret of all. The man, who due to his friendship with her parents, was able to spend many hours with the girl. The man who subjected the girl to sexual abuse for many years. He was not physically threatening; some would actually say he had been gentle. Yet, he forced the girl to experience things that were well beyond her years. This served to isolate her even more, served to fester the self-hatred and insecurity she felt. As the years went by, she carried this secret, afraid she wouldn't be believed if she told. Afraid she would feel even more alone, even more isolated if she told. Afraid to cause any commotion for fear she would lose acceptance of those around her. Afraid she would truly be alone.

I'm sure you have surmised by now that I am the little girl in the photograph. The image I've just given you of myself seems like a lifetime ago. I can barely remember that little girl. Yet, in some ways, I remember her like it was yesterday. I carry her with me everywhere I go. As much as I've tried to forget her, I find she has influenced everything I have ever done, every thought I have ever had. I have been through a lot with that little girl and I know she will always be with me. There have been years of depression, counseling, self-help books and just general miserable times. Sometimes, I thought I would never be happy. It seemed that at every turn those perceptions of myself that were formulated when I was that little girl held me back. They kept me from being happy. At times I thought I had overcome them, only to find them crop up again when I encountered an obstacle. That is, until I understood the purpose she served. Until I understood that through all those difficult times, I was searching. I was searching for relief from my feelings of inadequacy and relief from my self-imposed limitations. I was trying to find love for myself. I was trying to find something or someone who would fill the void I had within. The void created because I had developed no sense of self, no sense of my own worth. The void that was created because there had been no love directed there.

Due to the spiritual transformation brought about after the Kundalini activation, I had a new perspective on my life. I was able to see that because of the childhood I had, I was continually searching, trying to make things better, trying to help myself. This searching, this need to keep grasping, served as my reason to look within. It served as my catalyst for change. If people are satisfied with their lives, if everything has always gone smoothly for them, they have no reason to search; they have no reason to look further. But, if they have an obstacle to overcome, they can use that as a catalyst for self-understanding and for growth. In this way, I was able to begin looking at my childhood as an advantage, something I had been able to survive and learn from. It kept me searching for relief and understanding. It had served to point me in the direction I needed to go to find what lies within.

We do not all have such dramatic catalysts in our lives. This is because we do not all need them. We create the circumstances we need to learn and grow. For some, it may be as simple as trying to understand a fear of heights, then facing that fear. For others, such as myself, it may be necessary to experience great pain and difficulty repeatedly until we can understand and change it. A woman may remain with an abusive spouse through years of abuse. She does not heed the warnings of friends or family to leave. If finally she is able to break free, she repeats the pattern, again becoming involved with an abusive man. This is not an uncommon scenario. She repeatedly puts herself in the same situation until she is able to find the strength within herself, until she is able to find enough love and respect for herself to pull herself out of the situation and not allow herself to be victimized again. These are lessons she needs to learn and she keeps repeating them until she is able to learn what they were teaching her.

As I grew older I distanced myself from my family, particularly my mother. The years had mellowed her. My father passed away and she found herself in a different place. She now needed love from me. I tried to play the role of dutiful daughter, trying to make myself feel as a daughter should. I tried to find love inside to give her. I am not an uncaring person, quite the contrary. Perhaps, I care too much. Yet, each time I would extend myself to my mother, I unconsciously placed myself back in that place I had been in so many years before. I would again take on those perceptions of myself that I had grown up with. I was still striving to obtain that which I never had, the love and acceptance of my mother. It was as if all the years I had lived, the person I had become, the person with a beautiful family, successful career, that secure, loving and mature adult would all go right out the window. I would burst into tears the minute I left her house, feeling like that little girl again. Logically, this made no sense. It was ludicrous that I was still so affected by this woman, still so haunted by that which I had strived so hard to overcome. I realize now that it was I who allowed these early perceptions to haunt me. I alone had control over how I felt. She was unable to "make" me feel like anything I did not allow myself to feel. It is a hard lesson to learn that we alone are responsible for our feelings, emotions and circumstances.

I am not unusual. Many people carry things inside that they would like to forget. We all have things within us that cause us pain, things that we have had to deal with at various times throughout our lives. Sometimes, they are too painful to face. They make us uncomfortable. They cause us to feel weak. We put up all kinds of roadblocks trying to avoid dealing with them. We ignore them and try to forget them. We can go for years like that, until one day, there they are again. If you recognize yourself in these words, realize this is your catalyst for change. This is the thing that you need to face up to. You need to understand it and then finally integrate it into your being. This is the only way you will truly be free from it. Your catalyst is there to teach you something. It won't go away until you have learned its lesson.

I am reminded of the story of the elephant that was born into captivity, born to work in the circus. He spent his early life chained to a post so he would not wander off into the nearby town. One day, after he had grown to adulthood, he was approached by a visiting elephant who had not been chained. The visitor asked him why he remained in one place all the time. The elephant replied that he was chained to the post and was unable to leave. When the visitor looked down he saw that the chain had been outgrown years before and that the post had grown rusty. The chained elephant could have easily left at any time. He was now strong and powerful, yet he still perceived himself as that little elephant who was held by the chain. It was only his continued perceptions of himself that kept him a prisoner, kept him from realizing what he now was.

We are like that elephant when we hold onto our limiting perceptions of ourselves. We are the ones who hold ourselves back, believing what someone once told us about ourselves; believing we are unworthy, unloved, incapable, buying into someone else's definition of who we are, and taking on other people's opinions and accepting them as our own. Just as the elephant had the power to break free from his limiting self-imposed perceptions, so do we. We can choose to define ourselves. We can listen to our own inner voices, our own guidance. We can learn to trust what we feel is right.

It has taken me a long time to break my own chains and to change my perceptions of myself that I've carried since childhood. As I now find myself assisting others through my workshops and private sessions, I see that because of my experiences, I am able to really understand the pain of others. I am able to know what they are going through and what they are facing. I know the pain, the fear, the helplessness and the doubt, for I have been there. Because of what I have been through, I have also learned compassion and empathy. I also know how hard it is to pull away from these things, to learn and grow from them and to use that growth for positive change. It is because of my own difficulties, because of my catalysts, that I can now be effective in assisting others.

By understanding that my childhood experiences had actually helped me grow and helped me become who I am today, I was able to see that little girl in a new light. When I looked back at her, it was not to try to forget her, to banish her from my life because she was too painful for me, instead, I mentally sent her love. I directed the love toward that part of me that was still that little girl. I extended to her what she needed, because I knew better than anyone what that was. In doing this, I was able to accept her for what she was. I was able to accept that part of myself. I understood that she was an important part of me, important to my growth and important to the person I was becoming. In this way, I integrated her into my being. I understood that this realization concluded my healing.

Perhaps it is time for you to accept the part of you that you reject and hide from. Know that you will never be free of it, it is part of you for a reason. By accepting it, acknowledging it and loving it, you will be able to join with it. You will then be whole. Your catalyst really is here to help you.

To take this understanding one step further, it is important to realize that we are not our experiences. The things that happen to us throughout our lives are situations that we create to learn and grow from. What we truly are resides at a higher place, our soul level. This is the place that was there long before you were born into this life and will remain long after you depart. All the things you have experienced, the perceptions you have about yourself, that identity you call personality or ego, they all are on the peripheral of your true self. When you understand this, it will be easier to let go of the perceptions you have let limit you. It will be easier to feel things and allow things to flow through you without fear because you will know you are much more than the body you occupy. You will no longer seek satisfaction or validation externally. You will know those things are not truly you, so they cannot truly satisfy. You will be able to find what you need within yourself. Open your heart to yourself, your soul awaits.

CHAPTER 10

Energy Follows Thought

HAVE YOU EVER WALKED INTO A ROOM and had a "bad" feeling? Have you ever been around someone who made you uncomfortable, and you couldn't put your finger on exactly why? Have you ever known anyone who seemed to bring everyone around them down, drawing them into their dark mood? In these situations you were being affected by their energy. Likewise, I'm sure you have known people who made you feel comfortable from the moment you met them. You also have known people who were joyful and their mood seemed to touch everyone they had contact with, as if it were contagious. In these situations, you were also being affected by their energy.

Think about yourself. You begin to have negative thoughts, you criticize yourself for something you forgot, or you look in the mirror and have a negative thought about what you see. In initiating these negative thoughts, you are creating your mood. You are creating your reality. Everything starts with thought. You have heard this statement when someone describes how new inventions or discoveries are made, but did you realize that your thoughts also affect you and all those around you immediately?

The energy field around your body is a direct reflection of your current mental, emotional and physical state. With each thought you are creating the world in which you live. You are creating your reality. For example, say you are on a train, taking a long trip. You are looking forward to some quiet time, and you brought a book you have wanted to read for six months. You just settle down and get comfortable, open your book, and a very talkative woman sits beside you. You immediately formulate the thought that this woman is going to ruin your trip. You just know you won't be able to relax and read now that she is sitting next to you. You try to ignore her, hoping she will get the hint, but she doesn't seem to. You keep your nose in your book, but are unable to concentrate and you finally close the book in frustration. You spend the rest of the trip sulking while you pretend to listen to this woman babble. You have created your reality. You have chosen to be unhappy. You have already told yourself this will be a miserable trip. You have decided this woman will not let you enjoy your book and you view her as insensitive. You spend the trip sulking, wishing it would end. You arrive at your destination in a foul mood and it carries over to the rest of your day. If instead, when the woman sat next to you and began talking, you looked up and politely spoke with her, leaving yourself open to the possibility that maybe she is someone you might enjoy talking to, you might have been pleasantly surprised. You may have discovered you had a lot in common and the conversation may have uplifted you both. However, once you had made this attempt and found that you did not enjoy her company, you could choose to politely excuse yourself from the conversation. You could firmly but kindly state that you had brought this book that you really wanted to read and then proceeded to do so. She would not be insulted—you had been polite to her, merely stating your intentions and then carrying them out. In this last scenario, both you and the woman were uplifted. You did not spend the trip in misery and you would have arrived at your destination in a much better mood. Each situation was exactly the same at the onset, yet when you chose to have positive thoughts, when you chose to enjoy the trip, you are able to accomplish this regardless of the outside influences. The only difference in the two above scenarios were your thoughts—your attitude and intention of what was going to happen.

I am a perfect example of this. I was once a total "stress ball," always pushing to go faster, always feeling as if I needed something to worry about. I didn't feel right if I didn't have several things going around in my head at once, all competing for my time and attention. I viewed my life as being full of work. There was the house that needed cleaning, the clothes that needed washing, the errands that needed to be done, the kids that needed help with homework, the bills I needed to pay, you get the idea. I viewed all these things as work that I *had* to do. They were things that I had to get done so I could do what I *wanted* to do. The problem was, there was never enough time left to do anything else. I was exhausted and unhappy. I felt my life was only work. In fact, I had a message posted on my refrigerator that stated "Life is not all work, it can't be." This sums up how I viewed my life at the time.

My life was what I perceived it to be—exactly what I had created. When I realized that I was creating this stress for myself, that I had control over how I perceived things and that I alone could change my thoughts, my life became happier. You may say that sounds fine, but you still had to clean the house, do the laundry, run the errands, etc. Those things didn't change. What changed was my attitude, my thoughts. When I looked at each thing that I perceived as work and evaluated it for what it was adding to my life, I was able to get out from under that "have-to" mentality. For instance, the house needed cleaning. Nothing terrible would happen if I didn't mop the floor today, or even this week. I was operating under the perception that I had created for myself that the house *had* to be clean at all times. When I realized that I *liked* the house to be clean, that I was more comfortable in the house when it was clean, I then realized that cleaning the house was something I *chose* to do. If time did not permit, or I really did not feel like doing it, I didn't. This was my choice. The same held true for the errands. I sorted out what I felt was a priority and what I had only *perceived* as having to be done now. When it came to things like the laundry, I stopped trying to take everything on myself. We women seem to do that a lot. I asked my family for help. I explained what I was feeling and that I could not continue to do all these things myself. I put myself first for a change (a very foreign idea for most of us) and stated what I needed. (I have since learned this is part of loving and honoring yourself, this is simply being kind to yourself.) This was no problem to them! They didn't mind pitching in. All I had to do was ask! They had not realized I was feeling this way as I had always just taken everything on myself. They reminded me that they had not requested this of me, nor did they expect it. In this way, I had control over my life and my time. I enjoyed my life more, not having to wait until I had free time to begin enjoying myself. My family benefited, too, because now I was more fun to be around and did not make them feel as if I were resenting them. By taking care of myself, I had also helped those around me. These changes came about only through changes in my own thoughts and perceptions.

This is played out over and over again in our daily lives. Try to monitor your thoughts for one day and try to count how many times you think negatively or expect the negative to happen. When you do, it usually does, because that is what you created with your thought. We really do create our own realities, and it all starts with your thoughts. Positive uplifting thoughts are much more potent than negative ones. Negative thoughts hold you back, bring you down and perpetuate themselves. Once you are in that downward spiral, it is difficult to bring yourself out. On the other hand, positive thoughts serve to uplift you and those around you, they feed off each other and therefore create a snowball effect.

You can also test others. When you are around a negative person, watch their words and monitor their negative comments. Then pay attention to yourself. How are you being affected by their negative thoughts? Are you being dragged down into the reality they have created? Remember, no one can cause you to feel any specific way. You have the power to control your thoughts and perceptions and therefore, your moods and emotions. You control your energy. Part of your evolution is to understand your energy and how it can be used to create the experience you wish.

Our thoughts give off energy vibrations. These are the vibrations that resonate within our body's energy field (aura). Negativity, such as being critical, judgmental, prejudicial, unkind or selfish, all lower your vibration. These thoughts affect your body's energy field, lowering the rate at which your energy is vibrating. These are dense vibrations. Alternately, positive thoughts such as kindness, unselfishness, openness, honesty and especially the directing of loving thoughts raises the rate at which your energy is vibrating. You have heard the saying "birds of a feather flock together." This is because we are attracted to people who have similar energy fields; that is, people who have similar thoughts, who see things in the same way. Their energy is vibrating at a rate that is compatible to ours. Like attracts like. You will naturally gravitate toward those who are similar in vibration to you, because it is uncomfortable for us to be around energy that is not compatible to ours.

It is well known that colors are vibrations. Red vibrates at a different frequency than blue, or green, or yellow. This is how colors affect our moods. The higher the vibration, the lighter the color. The lower the vibration, the darker the color. This is why we associate darkness with negative things. We say someone is in a "dark mood," or someone is "in the dark." We blame bad things on "the forces of darkness." In contrast, we associate white with purity and goodness. We speak of "coming out of the darkness into the light." We perceive God as coming "from the light." We are able to intuitively perceive these variances in vibration.

When a soul transitions to the other side, they will find themselves in the company of souls of like vibration. Their experience is directly related to the rate at which their energy is vibrating. They have created their own reality on the other side, as they did here. The highly evolved beings, or master teachers that come to us as guides, are vibrating at an extremely high rate and therefore are "from the light." They have evolved themselves, through their thoughts and actions and have achieved a high rate of vibration. As a soul continues to evolve and raise their vibration, as these beings of light have, they become lighter and less dense. They are then pure energy and ultimately join as one with the Whole that makes up the consciousness. They can direct the energy, which is what they are, in any way they desire. They wish the same for us and therefore offer us their help and assistance. It is in this way that they can continue to evolve. It is the same for all of us. Through helping other souls (people), we help them raise their vibration, and raise ours as well.

All this talk of energy fields, vibrations and positive thoughts is necessary for you to understand that you are responsible for where you are in life. It is necessary for you to realize that you can create what you want with your own thoughts. Once you understand how your thoughts affect your world and those around you, you will see that you do have power over what happens to you. You do this every day, every hour, every minute, with every thought and perception you have, regardless if you are aware of it or not. The key to understanding this process and the power of your mind is *realizing* you are doing it. You can reflect on your experiences and realize that you created them. You put yourself in that situation and created your moods with your perceptions and thoughts about a specific situation. It must be understood that every moment, without exception, you are creating your experience. Even in that moment of reflection, as you think back over your behavior and the circumstances surrounding an event, you are understanding them through your perceptions, which are created by your past experiences and your interpretation of them. What does this mean? It means there is no absolute truth, no ultimate *right* answer. There is no set of instructions that you can follow to produce the life you envision. You possess something better! You possess the ability to write your own set of instructions as you go, expanding them as you expand, evolving them as you evolve. The possibilities are endless because you are infinite. This is important, because it is in directing your thoughts that you can learn to manipulate your energy, your life force, to create what you want. If you view the universe as friendly, and expect good things to come to you easily, you will find it will be so.

I was given a lesson in the direction of energy shortly after I began to access the guidance of Ramsey. I was directed to stand in my backyard, facing a large tree. I then focused on sending energy to the tree. I would look at the tree and mentally direct the energy toward it.

I felt an immediate increase in my energy as well. I felt my heart center expand and pulsate rapidly within my chest. Just the act of mentally directing energy/love somewhere else (a person, animal or situation) increases your vibration. I felt this increase in vibration as an increase in the energy flowing through me. I was then instructed to stand in front of Clyde and again mentally send the energy toward him. He was standing about fifteen feet away at the time and gasped in surprise when he felt my energy field expand to that circumference. He was able to feel this energy tingling in his hands as they touched the outside of my aura. I was being taught to direct my energy. I did this all with a thought. You are doing this all the time. It doesn't matter if you feel it as I can, it works the same way.

This is what prayer is and that is why it works. We think of prayer as asking a higher power for something, either on our behalf or someone else's. When you pray, you are sending energy directly to the person you are praying for. As I walk down the street I will mentally do this and I am able to feel the energy increase within me as I draw more energy toward myself and then out to the other person. This flow of energy in response to prayer can also be seen clairvoyantly as an energy stream flowing from one person to another.

As I continued to work with the energy in this way, I noticed that the more I focused on positive uplifting and loving thoughts, the higher my vibration would rise and the more energy I could feel. I also noticed that if I became depressed, or began thinking negatively, I was unable to feel the energy. This is because the negative thoughts would lower my vibration, serving to close my energy centers. Using these cues, I was able to learn quickly how to change my thought patterns and perceptions to more positive, uplifting ones. Ultimately, the goal of raising our vibration is for our soul to evolve higher, so we may experience more.

There is a Catch 22 situation with regards to this increase in vibration—another example of how the universe works in perfect ways. You cannot increase your vibration to connect with the higher realms if you are not of pure intention. If you are not mentally and spiritually ready to handle the responsibility that comes with the increase in energy and have not expanded your awareness enough to understand the broader perspective or worked at changing your thought patterns and perceptions to that of a more loving, nonjudgmental person, it simply will not happen. It is not necessary for you to achieve this totally loving, nonjudgmental state on a continuous basis, but merely to be open and willing to move toward this goal. To evolve you must be willing to learn your lessons from your everyday life.

Your energy vibration not only affects you, but those around you. You know when you are speaking to someone in an uplifting way, or when you are speaking to them in a demeaning or careless way. You know how you feel after the exchange and you know how you have made them feel. From your exchange, you have had the chance to raise not only their energy (vibration) but yours too. If you speak to five people in an uplifting, empowering way, they will leave and go out into the world feeling uplifted, positive and good about themselves. They will in turn affect five more people and so on. Once we understand the powerful effect our thoughts and words have on ourselves and those around us and we are able to take responsibility for what we send out into the world, we would find the world and its people would be greatly healed. As the saying goes, "no man is an island." We all directly affect all we come in contact with and all we don't.

When we think of sending loving thoughts we think of sending them to others. But it is important to realize that you must also send them to yourself. What is happening on the outside is a direct manifestation of what is happening on the inside. If you are not feeling good about yourself, you are not feeling good about the world. You will be unable to project anything but negativity outward. This is why it is imperative that you love yourself. Accept yourself unconditionally. Sure, you have faults, we all do. Sure, you have made mistakes, we all have. So, you try to do better next time. Understand that you are doing the best you can. Realize that you are a good person. You need to extend the same understanding, forgiveness and compassion toward yourself as you would a small child. You are entitled to nothing less. If you treat yourself with kindness and love you will find it will pour out of you to those around you. If you stop being so judgmental and critical with yourself, you will also be less so with others. So send those loving thoughts, what do you have to lose?

CHAPTER 11

The Sixth Sense

THE SIXTH SENSE, WE ALL HAVE IT. Some refer to it as intuition. It is our most underdeveloped sense and it is perhaps the most misunderstood. I believe this sense is meant to be used equally, along with our other five senses. Ideally, we would rely on our sixth sense in certain situations, just as we rely on our sense of sight or smell, when they are most appropriate. Further, by utilizing it and developing it we begin to understand the nature of ourselves and the universe and we *evolve*.

So what is this sixth sense? Before my Kundalini activated, I thought of the sixth sense as something mysterious. The term "ESP," meaning Extra Sensory Perception sounded like make-believe, something to be joked about—not something that had a place in our daily lives. Now that I experience this sixth sense daily, I understand how handicapped we are by not utilizing and developing it. Just as the blind person develops a keen sense of hearing and smell, we have learned to compensate for our lack of intuition. Because we have not experienced it, we don't miss it or realize our disadvantage. But, we are at a disadvantage. By not giving credence to our feelings and inner perceptions we are ignoring the best part of ourselves. We are shutting out the link to our soul. The sixth sense, or intuition, is the language of the soul.

The perceptions received directly into my being, bypassing the usual avenues of input (eyesight, hearing, mental thought) are the very essence of the soul. This is the universal language. After we leave our physical bodies, we will still be experiencing. This experiencing will be through what we refer to as the sixth sense. When I communicate with those who have passed, the communication is possible because they are utilizing this ability. This comes naturally to them, because they no longer occupy a physical body and have no other means of conveying ideas and thoughts.

Webster's dictionary defines intuition as follows: *A perception or view; immediate apprehension of truth, or supposed truth, in the absence of conscious rational processes.* In light of that description, and given our society's tendency to discount anything that is not tangible or logical, it is no wonder we are conditioned not to rely on our intuition. A more fitting definition would be: *1) An understanding or direct knowing, received directly into conscious awareness, without the use of any known avenue of perception; or,* 2) *A means of acquiring understanding in the most direct, efficient way possible, bypassing the physical senses and connecting with the essence or core of everything in existence.* Not so mysterious, just an untapped part of our being that is not understood or accepted, because we do not fully comprehend what and who we are.

This has been my quest since the Kundalini activated, to understand how all these incredible experiences were possible. What did it mean when I could focus on something and instantly know and understand it? How was it possible for me to feel the emotions, feelings, illnesses and perceptions of anything and anyone I focused on? How can everyone tap into this wonderful experience? What would the world be like if everyone did have this experience and understood why they could? These questions have kept me searching for understanding and these questions have led me to write this book, to share what is possible and to make evident the reality and potential that lies within each one of us. Psychic phenomena is not unexplainable or mysterious, it is just not yet understood or experienced by enough people. *This is within all of us!* It is normal for us to tap into our source and each other. It is the undeniable and unstoppable forward thrust of our evolution as a species to discover and experience these things.

The people of ancient Greece used to believe in various gods to explain the workings of life. An elaborate mythology was created to explain what was not understood. Now that we understand why the sun comes up and why the weather changes, these things are not mysterious and the mythology has dropped away. The same will happen with our ideas regarding psychic phenomena and our untapped human potential.

I would like to explain what my intuitive perceptions feel like so you can begin to recognize them in yourself. We do all have them. The trick is to trust them. This is probably the hardest part, especially at first. So many people come to me with questions for which they already know the answers. They just don't trust what they feel. They want some reassurance and confirmation before they will give credence to their inner direction.

When I do a reading for someone, I simply focus on them and blank my mind, dropping any expectations. This is done quickly. If we were facing each other, you would not be able to notice that I had done anything. (This came very naturally, it was not something I had to study to learn to do. Through practice, I became more proficient at blanking my mind, but the know-how seems to be pre-wired within us.) Impressions begin to flow in, sometimes so quickly that I have to slow them down by momentarily closing my mind to them. When this happens, I usually redirect my inner question to more specific terms. I need to look at one thing at a time because I am not able to interpret (put into words) what I am receiving if too much comes too fast. It is like hearing many voices in your head and not being able to hear any one voice distinctly.

For instance, a client may ask about her husband. As I focus on him, I may receive everything at once, his personality traits, his childhood, his relationships and his job. I usually ask the client to be more specific in what she wants me to look at. Perhaps she is concerned about his health. I then direct my focus to his health and I receive only that information. Sometimes, this will bring other things to me—if there is a connection. Say his health problem is a result of stress from his job, the information that comes to me would follow a chain. First, I would receive the impression of how he feels, then I would ask why, and receive the impression of his feeling stress and from there I would follow the stress to the root. When I receive the impression of his job, it would come with a feeling of why he felt stressed there. Maybe a supervisor was giving him trouble, or he was just bored and tired, or disgruntled with the pay or conditions. All this happens in a matter of seconds. It is cumbersome to explain using the written word, but all these understandings come in seemingly at once. I have no awareness of any interpretation between receiving the impressions and understanding their meaning.

I have been amazed at the "perfectness" of this type of communication. When I receive an impression, there is an immediate knowing and understanding. There is a smoothness that is unhampered by the limitations of language and vocabulary. In fact, I have found the most difficulty lies in trying to verbalize what I receive for my clients. Sometimes, very complex ideas and complicated emotions are received in an instant with complete understanding; however, to sort them out and put them into words always leaves me recognizing the inadequacy of verbal communication. With words we can only communicate one idea at a time. It is very much like translating from one language to another. Sometimes there are no literal translations for the idea you are trying to convey so you find yourself using many different words, dancing around the meaning, but never finding the word that will convey the exact meaning you are trying to get across.

Most information comes to me through these feelings and impressions. Sometimes, clairvoyant images (a picture in my mind) accompany a feeling. The image usually is symbolic and has meaning to me, triggering a recognition within me, enabling me to better interpret information for the client. When I communicate with those who have passed, it is common for me to see whatever word (a necklace, a pet, a flower) they are trying to convey. When I am reading someone who is still in the physical body it is more common for me to only receive feelings and impressions. Sometimes, when I continue asking something, looking for clarification, I will receive a clairvoyant image to drive home the point.

I have mentioned before that you need to trust your feelings. Your feelings are the key. They are the means by which we experience our soul. Feelings are experienced via the nervous system, which is the link between the physical body and the energetic essence that is the soul. Feelings, in this context, are not to be confused with emotions. Emotions are intertwined with thoughts. Emotions change with thoughts. Emotions are what we create and experience when we add thought to feelings. Feelings, in their pure form, are an inner guidance, a way of experiencing something directly, bypassing (coming before) the physical senses. Feelings come before thoughts.

The mind is not the center of our intelligence. I remember a time when we had a new puppy in the house. We were keeping a sharp eye on him during the housebreaking period and as we sat in the living room one evening I realized he wasn't anywhere in sight. I was exhausted from the day and didn't want to get up and search the house for him. Instead, I turned my focus on him, opening to feel what he was feeling. I immediately felt as if I had to go to the bathroom and I had a sense of "looking." I realized he was looking for a place to do his business and I quickly ushered him outside. My husband looked at me, gestured to his head with his finger and said, "You need to use these abilities more often." This struck me as strange because his gesture of pointing to his head implied that my intuitive abilities are centered in my mind. Actually, when I intuit something, I feel the center as being in my heart area (also known as the heart chakra). My mind is totally excluded from this process. If I do engage thought or emotion while using my intuitive senses, it disrupts the process and I cannot trust what I receive. The mind may be the center of our intellect, but it is not the center of our intelligence or the core of our essence.

As I questioned the connection between the nervous system and our perceptual abilities, I received the following understanding: The entire body has intelligence and this intelligence is the energy that directs the universe and everything in creation. The body and mind are one cohesive unit, and function as such. Energy is the transmitter between all life. Physical matter springs forth from the explosion of subatomic particles and the atom is formed. This process is energy changing form. When a soul is to be born into the physical plane, the conscious awareness (soul) that carries with it the energy/impressions from many lifetimes seats itself into the new body and as it once again anchors its awareness on the physical plane, energy has changed form. The awareness (soul) merges into the physical body, connecting itself to this physical world, yet maintains the energetic connection via the body's nervous system. The nervous system transmits electrical impulses (energy) throughout the entire body and is the "bridge" that unites the physical and nonphysical planes.

Those with sensitive nervous systems feel things more deeply than others. They usually have more sensitive physical bodies as well. An intolerance for alcohol and medication is common. The skin can also reflect this sensitivity. For me, simply scratching an itch will leave red welts, sometimes lasting hours. In meeting with people, I find these things are common among those who have sensitive nervous systems. Most of these people have had some degree of psychic experience, usually going back to childhood.

Those with sensitive nervous systems have *highly evolved* nervous systems. That is, they are a soul that has reached a relatively high level of awareness in previous lifetimes. Sometimes, we call this an "old soul." These people tend to have difficult lives. It is said that the most growth is experienced by those who have difficult lives and it is speculated that such difficulty was planned to enable the soul to experience a lot of growth during a lifetime. In actuality, those people with sensitive nervous systems are having such difficulty adjusting to living in the physical world because they experience great inner conflict. They feel this connection within their bodies, but with no understanding or point of reference, they are at a loss to explain it. When they begin to experience a physical life again and attempt to fit into the world, it goes against their inner truth—that inherent wisdom that they brought with them. They are not aware of the source of the conflict and they continue to search for relief. When enough maturity and experience is obtained during a lifetime, the individual is able to reconnect with their inner guidance and draw forth the soul's accumulated wisdom. A commonality I have observed in the course of my work is that this searching kicks in around age thirty-five or forty. A lifetime of questions usually comes to a head, demanding attention.

Everyone, sensitive nervous system or not, has experienced this connection to their soul. Whenever you have goose bumps or chills when hearing something that touches you deeply, you are experiencing a direct connection to your soul. Sometimes, just an act of synchronicity will evoke this type of physical response. A passing chill, a gasp of breath or a tingling sensation that catches you by surprise—these are bodily responses, brought to you via your nervous system, as your soul was touched by something you experienced. Follow these sensations, pay attention and don't dismiss them. This is your soul, speaking to you.

CHAPTER 12

Direct Knowing

PERHAPS MORE IMPORTANT TO MY individual growth than experiencing the psychic abilities previously discussed has been what I refer to as "direct knowing." I use this term to describe the process of asking for understanding about something and then receiving it directly, in the same way I receive intuitive information. This fascinates me and early in this experience my husband and I would stay up all night, asking questions and receiving answers. Questions about the nature of things, the nature of man, the connectedness of life, the soul essence, reincarnation, God, you name it, we asked it. Sometimes the understandings would come as a whole clump of ideas. Other times, I would receive clairvoyant images to explain what I was trying to understand. Many times I would receive an example, put in very simple terms as a way to explain a complicated concept. We found that our minds, with their perceptions of individuality and separation, were sometimes unable to comprehend the full meaning of the information I would receive. At times I felt totally inadequate, lacking the knowledge or vocabulary I needed to verbalize the impressions I was receiving. I remember feeling that there was so much in here but so little I could express so others could understand.

As with everything that has happened to me, I wanted to know how this was possible, I wanted to know how it worked.

I received the following understandings in response to those questions: As you reach for understanding you send out energy vibrations that are received by all levels of the consciousness. Whichever level is appropriate is the level that responds. This is not responding as you perceive, such as thought consciously initiating the correct response. It is more like something that automatically happens, much like your body digests food without your conscious instruction to do so. It is simply being itself, doing what it does and nothing else is required. If someone wants to bring something to themselves, the universe responds. This is the mirror-effect of the universe. What you focus on, expands. What you fear, you experience. That is why your thoughts surrounding the avoidance of painful emotions or experiences only bring you more of the same thing you are trying to avoid. With those thoughts or strategies, you are in essence creating and drawing to you what you wish to avoid. This is why it is the strategies around the avoidance and clinging, not the painful emotions or experiences themselves, that ultimately are responsible for your suffering.

When one transcends the individual limitation in perception, there is an understanding that whatever flows to and from anywhere, or whatever flows to and from anyone, is all part of the same Whole. There is no reason to ask or even desire to know who asked and who received. This is because the Whole is one cohesive unit, one being, connected through the energy/consciousness that is the Source. When a being has evolved to perceive himself as this Whole, there is an extension of everything available to him. This is an extension of himself. When he leaves his current physical human body, it *is* him. This extension is the body of knowledge, or *direct knowing* that exists from everything in existence (All That Is). Because this body of knowledge is constantly changing and interacting with everything else, there is never a time when just one question is being asked and only one is being answered.

Try to release your current perceptions as I lead you through this example: The body of the whole responds to itself in the same way you respond to your body. If your toe itches, you scratch it. You do not stop to ask if the toe asked to be scratched or if you should respond with the scratch. This is not necessary because you do not view the toe as being separate from yourself. From your present reality, your toe is part of you. Yet, if your spouse said their back itched, they would tell you so and you would respond by scratching it. From your present reality, you and your spouse are separate.

In the consciousness, there is no perception of separation. All parts are viewed as the toe—merely other portions needing something—to which it responds automatically. This response is not the response of something separate from you (a guide) sending you what you asked for. There is no judgment or decision by something other than yourself, deciding if you deserve what you have asked for. It is the automatic, inherent reaction from the Source, responding to itself in the way you would respond to any portion of your body.

The Source flows constantly through everything. Every thought that is placed into existence by you reverberates throughout the consciousness. As all thoughts interact and blend, a general direction is created. This is how mass consciousness is formed. The outward manifestations of this are reflected through society's phases, moods, changing opinions and attitudes.

You may ask if your thoughts or requests are automatically registered, why do you not receive what you ask for? The popular explanation is that you are not ready for it, or that you have somehow blocked it from happening. What is actually occurring is that whenever you act in a way that is inconsistent with your soul, that is, goes against and takes you farther from its purpose (the self-realization of yourself as All That Is) you are sending conflicting signals to the universe. What you are is the soul that yearns to return to the ocean of consciousness. That is what all your lifetimes have been about. When you are unaware of that purpose and you divert from that path, you are unable to understand and comprehend the response from the universe. It is a two-way street. Since there is no separation, it is not just you sending out questions and desires to the universe and expecting to receive something directly back just for you.

You are not lesser than any other part. You are an equal part of the Whole. As such, you are constantly receiving and interacting with all that exists. When a being transcends the ego level and opens to other aspects of itself, there is constant contact and interaction with everything else. This is not on an individual basis, although it can be perceived that way from the human perspective. It is actually your tapping into the consciousness or direct knowing in much the same way a sponge reacts in water. The sponge, being totally immersed in water, absorbs what it can hold, expands, then contracts according to its level of need at the time. You are like the sponge, drawing into your being what you need for expansion. You cannot say which part of the water was responding to you, nor can you say which part you asked to respond, only that you received what you needed from the whole body of water.

As you continue to expand your awareness and understanding, you are able to feel everything within the Whole as part of you (like you now view your toe). With this comes the inherent ability of your being to just *know* what it needs. You can understand this in terms of your body. You just *know* what your body needs. You know when you need rest, you know when you need food or you know when a relationship is not good for you. If you no longer perceived your body at the human ego level, but expanded to perceive yourself as the Whole, you would respond in the same way to everything within the Whole, just as you now do to everything within your human body. When you are integrated with higher consciousness, direct knowing will allow you to respond to all aspects of yourself (other people, animals, etc.) spontaneously, without prior thought of what is needed, or what is proper. You will just *know* what is needed and you will just provide it—not because you want to help them individually, but because you will perceive them as you and you will be respond-ing to a need within your body. This is the ease of existence that highly evolved beings enjoy.

Since you have not yet expanded your perception to in-clude what lies beyond your human body as part of you, you are unable to grasp or consciously sense what you may be receiving back from the universe. When your requests and desires take you further from your soul's purpose (the self-realization of yourself as the One or All That Is), you are not able to draw to yourself that which is not in alignment with this purpose. It is very much like your toe requesting that you sever it at the joint, or that you turn it into a finger. These requests are certainly not going to be answered by you be-cause you know your toe is a toe and it is not going to serve you or the toe if you respond to these requests.

In the instance of your ego making requests that are not in alignment with your soul or your ultimate purpose for be-ing, the understanding can be made that the universe works in perfect ways because it is inherently perfect. All that is encom-passed within it allows for further experience and awareness of itself. All parts within the whole, being equal, have the same integrity within the Whole. You, being a point within that Whole are free to experience yourself as anything you wish, for as long as you wish. The other points work with you, as you do with them, to allow this experience (be it perceived as good or bad). This is done quite unconsciously without the need for intellect to direct any aspect of this interaction.

There is no separate interaction between you and other parts, nothing outside of yourself that you are to aspire to. From within the human paradigm of illusional separation, it is difficult to grasp this concept. Your sensory perception tells you that you are a separate being. Through your expansion you will come to know yourself as more than what the senses show you. As this happens, you will rely less and less on the senses and rely more and more on the *direct knowing* that is coming from within you.

As you continue to expand your awareness, you will no-tice you receive direction from "out of the blue." You may be trying to grasp something and suddenly, after you have stopped trying to intellectually grasp it, you receive the *knowing* you were searching for. This understanding will suddenly just be there, without your conscious knowledge of how it got there. This is *direct knowing* and it is the way in which beings ex-pand themselves. This is also the way beings communicate, beyond the language used by any physical form or species. For one cohesive unit to exist, there must be some form of unification, of awareness of all its parts. This direct knowing is sometimes called intuition and it exists within all beings, whether realized or not. Direct knowing expands as you evolve and continues to enable you to grasp that which seems just out of reach.

From deep within the ocean, there is no idea of which molecule of water rose up into a wave or spread onto the sand. The ocean is one cohesive unit. There is no perception of separation between its water molecules. When a river emp-ties itself into the ocean it ceases to be a river and then be-comes part of the ocean. It can no longer be identified as a river. As you continue to expand your awareness, you will come to identify with the ocean, rather than the river. During this expansion, you will discover, through direct knowing, what you need to do at any particular moment and in any particular situation. This direct knowing will not come from any teacher, book or workshop, it can only come from within you.

CHAPTER 13

Becoming Whole

BECOMING WHOLE MEANS ENDING the experience of separation. It means ending the experience of separation from each other, from our planet, from the universe and from the truth of our being. Becoming whole is the process of bringing our physical experience and mental awareness into alignment with all of creation. Enlightenment is the *direct experience* of knowing oneself to be All That Is, not separate from anyone or anything. *Being* whole is the stabilization of this direct experience in your mind/body, bringing with it radiant health, immense inner peace and well being, blissful joy and happiness, deep inner wisdom and underlying love for everything in existence. To experience this directly, through this physical vehicle we call our body, is the purpose for our existence.

Aligning mind, body and spirit is a matter of understanding your perceptions, (the power of your mind) and erasing all perception of separation. The beliefs you have about yourself are everything. The experience you have is dictated by *who you think you are*. This is the magic. This is the secret we all seek. Everything is directed by thought, which is energy.

We all are on a path, a path to discover who we really are. That discovery is preceded by many lifetimes of searching, learning and experiencing. Mainly, these experiences serve to teach us who we are not. Through the depths of depression, through fear and repression, through physical illness and suffering, struggle after struggle, we slowly learn that we alone control everything we experience. This discovery leads us to understand our divinity and our part in all of creation.

I have had the opportunity to counsel many people who are seeking spiritual answers. Through my body and mind, I have felt their pain, their fears, their emotions and their potential. There is always an issue they carry with them in their aura (energy field surrounding the body) that has formed their primary experience. This is usually a belief about themselves formed in childhood, handed down from family or society, or brought forward from a past life. In understanding this belief, and accepting that it is only a thought, holding no basis in reality, they are a little nearer to understanding their true nature. In overcoming their self-imposed limitations and fears by changing their belief of who they think they are, they come to understand they hold all the answers they seek.

As we seek to become whole, we must understand that all parts of our being must be included. As we follow our inner knowing along our path and seek to understand our existence, there must be the recognition that everything is interconnected. As we look for answers to aid in our healing, we must understand that our physical illnesses are not just "of our body" and that our mental conflicts are not just "of our minds." We must understand that we cannot treat the physical body as a set of symptoms, as our medical doctors do, nor can we assume that our mental and emotional conflicts are solely caused by mental attitudes and perceptions, as our psychiatrists and psychologists do. We are integrated beings and we must consider ourselves as such. Any other approach to health, happiness, education or fulfillment results in imbalance and disorganization of our vital energy.

For any imbalance to exist, there must first be the experience of separation from our soul. The soul is always in perfect harmony with all of creation. This is our nature. Through our lives, our beliefs and our actions, we experience a separation from our soul. For most of us on the earth today, this means

our entire lives (indeed, the entire lives of previous generations) have been spent living in the experience of this separation and the subsequent search to find peace, health and happiness (to again live in alignment with our true selves). The
problems that plague mankind and the earth today are a direct
result of this experience of separation.

The experience of separation can be described as the
absence of the feeling of having a center from which we derive our direction and inner peace, which becomes our normal
state when we become realigned. The experience of separation results in an energetic imbalance which is felt in every
aspect of our being. This imbalance is the root cause of the
mental conflict and difficulty we experience. It is the reason
we live in unnatural ways, unknowingly abusing our bodies
with unnatural food, toxins and conditions. It is the reason we
experience physical illness and disease and it is the reason we
don't recognize what should be readily apparent. The experience of living in misalignment from our soul perpetuates itself
as our actions and thoughts serve to keep us in this state of
unnatural existence. The collective consciousness we have created, based on living in the experience of separation, continues to take us farther away, as individuals, as a society, as a
species and as a planet.

The imbalances in our physical bodies are a result of not
living in accordance with the laws of nature, with our true
selves. This physical imbalance exists long before we realize
or experience physical symptoms of illness. As the imbalance
grows, physical symptoms appear and come to our attention.
At this point, a physician may say an illness is "all in your
head." The imbalance is manifesting itself as an illness within
your body, the symptoms appearing at your weakest point but
have yet to advance to the point where medical science can
detect their presence (and give a name to the symptoms)
through standard testing procedures. This is your soul, acting
through your body, sending out signals to get your attention.
You are going farther away from your soul, you are not living

in ways that harmonize your bodies (physical, mental and emotional) and you are physically suffering from this separation. If the root cause is not eliminated, these symptoms will continue to worsen and a name (disease) will be given to your symptoms.

When we experience mental conflict and emotional problems, these are not merely psychosomatic, that is, existing only in our mind. Our minds are not separate from our bodies. The body is the physical manifestation of our mental experience. Much of the mental conflict and suffering that is so much a part of our everyday lives is a result of our self-created mental perceptions and attitudes which have been born from the systematic imbalances of our bodies. We have been futilely trying to obtain physical health, emotional happiness and mental well-being while living in a body that is in a state of imbalance. There can be no mental peace and well-being while the body is toxic and unbalanced.

Your mental and emotional mood is felt in your body. Your body responds to your emotions, even in the simplest of functions (i.e., digestion, reproduction, blood flow and physical healing). Likewise, the way your body feels directly dictates your state of mind. When your body is pure, detoxified and thriving in a state of vibrant, natural health, there is a clarity of mind and a feeling of well-being that is beyond description to those who have not experienced it. The mind/body are working in perfect cohesion, functioning as one unit. This realignment of your mind/body will automatically connect you with your spirit, your soul. You will feel this connection within your physical body and sense this unity deeply within your conscious awareness. This is the experience of being whole and through this wholeness you can further expand to touch parts of yourself previously unknown.

As we go about our lives, creating our experiences through our thoughts and reaping the results through our physical bodies, we set up the means by which we can recognize our interconnection to all things. In this way, we can once again be directed by our inner voice and by following it, be realigned with our soul. To truly understand this concept, you must first look to yourself and directly experience within your mind/ body the cause and effect of your thoughts and actions. There is no area, which this is more apparent than the reaction of your physical body to your actions, choices and thoughts. It is important to note, however, that the onset of physical illness is not to be viewed in a linear way—that is, to believe that your thoughts alone create an imbalance in your body, thus manifesting a physical illness. This has been a popular stance by some alternative healers in the new age movement. What is actually happening is occurring simultaneously. This is because you are an organic being, subject to the physical laws of nature. For an illness to be experienced, there must be physical conditions within the body to facilitate the symptoms. This is not to say that these physical conditions must exist in the body *before* the corresponding mental attitudes any more than the mental attitudes must exist *before* the physical symptoms can be manifested. This is a "which came first, the chicken or the egg" question. The answer is not that clear cut. Both mind and body act simultaneously. Most people are not aware of this because they cannot immediately feel the results of their thoughts or actions within their bodies due to the density, decreased sensitivity and energetic blockages created by the toxicity in their cells, tissues and organs. When your body is detoxified, you will be more easily able to feel your physiological functions and experience the movement of your thoughts (energy) through your body. This awareness is necessary for your progression and mastery of this world of physical matter.

Throughout this experience of living in separation from our true selves we have been living blindly. Our choices have not been in harmony with our soul. Therefore, they have not been in accordance with the planet, our fellow humans or other life. We have been living in ways that go against what is natural for us. I am not referring specifically to our individual choices made consciously during our lifetime. We have not been aware of the ramifications and consequences of the un-natural choices which have been passed down and followed, because they have seemed the norm for generations. We have unknowingly been following what we have been taught. The beliefs and expectations of society and our culture dictate the lives we lead and so it has been continued, this experience of separation, generation after generation.

The path to realignment is twofold. First, the body must be detoxified by a return to natural living, including a natural, whole foods diet. Through this detoxification, your body will correct imbalances and heal any damage that has not gone beyond the degenerative stage. As your body cleanses and heals, you will experience many revelations and changes that will demonstrate to you the unrealized potential at your disposal. When you change what you put into your body, your body changes to match the vibration of what is ingested. This in turn affects your mood, your attitudes and your thought process. This change in frequency affects your perception, allowing you to perceive the larger reality of which you are a part. We will discuss this connection more fully in Part III.

This step cannot be bypassed. Without it, you will not have the direct experience necessary to transcend the ingrained beliefs and traditions which have held us for so long. Without it, you will still be living in a state of experienced separation between your mind and body and your soul.

Second, you must release those issues (beliefs) that have kept you in the experience of limitation. These include any self-limiting doubts, negative feelings about yourself and feelings of hopelessness and fear. You must understand the process by which you create your own experiences and learn to use the wonderful and Divine power of your mind to create the reality you want.

Part III

Experiencing

It is only when we forget all our learning
that we begin to know.
　　　　　　　　　　—Henry David Thoreau

.

CHAPTER 14

The Basics—Your Physical Body

THOSE OF YOU WHO ARE READING this book are on a spiritual path or you wouldn't be drawn to this type of information. I know your desire is to tap into the same abilities I have and to share these experiences. This is my most sincere wish for you, to directly feel who you are from within. Once that happens, you will need nothing else, nature will take its course and you will grow at an accelerated rate in the perfect order of the universe.

In this section, we will discuss various things you can do to help with your opening. I have given a lot of thought to which things I could share that would prove most useful to those on the spiritual path who may be trying to activate their intuitive abilities and open to Divine guidance. I have included those things that have become obvious as my body changed and my perceptions expanded.

The first area that demands attention is the physical body. The following quote by Swami Satchindananda sums it up beautifully: *Your first duty is to make the body healthy. Without health, nothing can be achieved. Not only higher goals, but even worldly success is based on your health, your condition. Whatever you want to do, spiritual, social, national, you have to do it with your body. Your thoughts are manifested only through your body. You can fulfill desires only through your body.*

This is so overlooked! To align body, mind and spirit you must first understand that no separation exists between these three aspects of your being. We tend to view the physical body as separate from the mind and vice versa. We consider our spiritual nature as separate from our physical existence, as if spirituality is something that exists beyond our physical reality. We have viewed these aspects separately, as if we could bypass one to experience the other. I have noted, through my intuitive sessions, that the majority of clients have no concept of the connection between their physical body (its condition, their diet) and the spirituality they are so intently seeking. These people are devoting vast amounts of time to learning various alternative healing modalities, developing their intuitive abilities and practicing various modes of meditation. Even among people that we consider to be spiritually knowledgeable and health conscious, there seems to be a predominance of ignorance regarding the role the physical body plays in their search for enlightenment. Most people do not connect their diet to their inability to meditate, to their level of inner peace or to their potential to grasp the expansion of consciousness they seek. Most people only perceive their bodies to be affected by their diet to the extent their health is affected. They feel trapped by their body and discount the very message that is being conveyed. They may make changes in diet and lifestyle when their health suffers, but since they cannot see or feel their soul, they are not aware that the physical pain and discomfort they feel in their physical body is also felt through their mental and emotional bodies and into the awareness that is their soul.

I will repeat for clarification—there is no separation between your physical body and your soul. These are two energies, differing in vibrational level, interconnected and dependent upon each other. You are not "other than your soul" and you are not "other than your body." Nothing exists autonomously. Everything you do to your body affects your mind, therefore your attitudes, behavior and perceptions. Further, your state of mind affects what you do to your body. Your thoughts, actions and moods resonate within your aura and radiate, through your subtle bodies, to your spirit. A cycle of cause and effect is set into motion with each choice you make, a cycle that can be difficult to break until you understand that you created it and you can change it.

The physical body is simply another form the energy takes. You are, literally, energy that is conscious. Your physical body is this energy, which has become denser and currently holds your awareness, anchored in your body, to the physical plane. Our bodies are not empty shells that can be discarded or ignored. They are not hollow vessels that our spirit jumps into at birth and jumps out of at death. They are living manifestations of the energy that we are. When we die, the energy simply changes form, becomes less dense and exists as pure awareness, existing without a physical body.

Your body contains the inherent intelligence of the universe. *The kingdom of God is within you* (Luke 17:21). *Know ye not that ye are the temple of God, and that the Spirit of God dwelleth in you* (I Cor. 3:16)? It is through your body that you can tap into this intelligence. Your nervous system is the "bridge" which transmutes the energy down to the density of your body. The nerves spread throughout the body, carrying energy vibrations to every cell, literally feeding the body with energy. The nervous system is a direct link to the higher awareness of your soul. The purer your body, the clearer your connection, it's that simple.

Our bodies are not just organic life forms and biological specimens made up of various physiological systems. Science has examined them and understands the mechanics and operations of the body, but since only the physical and tangible aspect of the body is seen, it is still viewed as an autonomous machine. Nothing could be farther from the truth! Our bodies are in existence within our consciousness, because of our consciousness, created by our consciousness, for the purpose of allowing our consciousness to experience the density of physical matter. Our bodies are conscious energy, in the form of physical matter.

You are this energy. This is important to understand. The energy is not something that is separate from you. It is not something that you bring through your physical body from outside of yourself. We need to dissolve the perception of the energy being separate from us, something we bring through our bodies, something that we want to open up to and experience. Rather, we are the energy, our bodies are the physical matter resulting from the concentration of energy and to evolve we need to view ourselves as energy, thus breaking the paradigm that holds us to the limitations of the physical body.

Your physical body is what holds your current awareness, your current reality. Rather than trying to transcend it (which may allow for fleeting, temporary experiences of the larger whole), it is necessary to use the physical body as your vehicle to experience your true self. To look only to the mind for expansion of your awareness may allow for some experiences of what lay beyond, but, to truly evolve you must anchor this awareness into your everyday life and experiences. Many people get caught in this trap. They meditate for long periods of time and experience transcendental states and energetic experiences, which disappear when they return to the "real world." Some choose to retreat from the world in an attempt to hold onto and isolate these experiences into their everyday reality. They have unknowingly created a separation between their spiritual life and the real world. To dissolve this boundary, you must embrace the physical part of yourself and realize that your physical existence itself *is* spiritual. Your body is the vehicle through which you will first discover, then experience the larger part of yourself, the Divine Source within. Your body is the vehicle that will take you there.

All this discussion of the importance of your physical body in realizing your true self and coming into alignment with your soul is necessary because this is the area in which we have strayed the farthest from what is natural. You must understand that above all else, what you do to your body (what you eat, how you care for your body) affects what you experience. *You are only capable of clarity of thought, positive attitude, pureness of action or harmonic physical existence to the extent your body can allow.* When you are trying to reach beyond and experience the inner knowing of your soul, you will only be able to do so to the level and extent you have allowed your body to take you. You cannot possibly perceive or comprehend what lies beyond your current level of awareness until you experience it yourself. You cannot experience it yourself until your body is returned to its natural state. You are the master of your vehicle. You must direct it where to take you. If you wish to arrive at your destination, you must provide the proper care and maintenance. You determine your body's condition, ability and current potential through the choices you make.

As your body is allowed to purify itself, the transformation that takes place is that of a perfectly whole, wonderfully elaborate, yet simplistic organism, being allowed to function as it was intended. In this return to natural functioning, there is a wonderful sense of well-being that will overcome you, as if all is right with the world. As your body returns to balance, all truly is right with the world because the energy that you produce with your thoughts and actions will be in alignment with the universe. You will be capable of experiencing an inner connection that was there all along, but was previously outside your range of perception.

Through this transformation, you will discover that your physical body is actually a Divine vehicle, which you occupy for the purpose of discovering your own divinity. This revelation is apparent when you observe the inherent wisdom of the body as you experience first hand the natural processes (physical, mental and emotional), which ensue as you allow your body to return to its natural state. When you let nature take its course, without interference, the inherent wisdom and perfect order which exist within you is revealed to you. This is a leap of faith for most of us raised in the West. We were influenced by the current allopathic medical industry and the pharmaceutical companies, which have imparted to us a psychological dependence and belief that the body's natural functions need to be "treated." We have learned to look at normal bodily functions such as birth and menopause as conditions that need outside assistance. We have mislabeled and misunderstood the body's natural healing functions as diseases that need to be "cured." We have been taught what we should eat by the industries who profit from our consumption, instead of looking to nature and following what our bodies demonstrate to us.

There is a universe of knowledge and understanding that we are meant to receive from and through our bodies. This knowledge and understanding is not about science or the mechanical workings of our organs. This knowledge will not be found or understood through poking, prodding, testing, injecting, cutting, radiating or altering in any way. This is higher knowledge and it can only be directly experienced and observed when we take a leap of faith and trust our inner truth. Your body has a lot to show you about who you are. There is much you can learn about creation and your place in it from the natural processes that will be revealed to you as you purify your physical body. By allowing the body to function as nature intended, it will restore balance and health and further demonstrate to you that you truly are interconnected to everything in creation.

CHAPTER 15

The Separation

SINCE OUR PHYSICAL BODIES ARE the vehicles from which to experience our higher existence and the bridge through which our inner wisdom and guidance is felt, why is it we are all searching for ways to hear? Something so natural and inherent to our existence and continued spiritual evolution should be obvious. Our connection shouldn't be obscured from our awareness. This is our birthright and it is something other life forms take for granted as part of simply being alive.

How did we become so cut off from our essence? Why doesn't everyone feel the energy and the universal intelligence and guidance flowing through his being? Why are we looking for answers outside ourselves, when the only answers are to be found inside? Why is it so hard to hear? And, why do we even need to ask these questions?

I have received many images to help me understand concepts for which I had no frame of reference. Images do not rely on words, which are very limiting. Images tell a story and for our linear minds, they depict understandings that cannot be obtained through words. To further your understanding, I will now share some of these images with you: Visualize a target with a bull's-eye and rings radiating outward from the center. The bull's-eye, or center, represents the One (the Self, God, the Consciousness). This is where there is no individual and no perception of dualism. From this point, all is known and understood. This is "home" where we all seek to return. As we venture out from the center, we are getting farther from home and the farther we go outward, the harder it is to see, feel or know anything that was very clear when we were in the center. The more people who venture out into the rings, the more momentum this outward gravitation has and the harder it is to return to the center. The more thoughts there are that are entrenched in the limited awareness of the outer rings, the farther it spirals outward. This is the collective consciousness that is creating the current awareness.

As you get closer to the center, you are able to recognize what is truth, because that is home. The closer you come to the center, the more you are able to feel, hear and know from within what it is that will bring you even closer to the center. Once one is already out in one of the rings as the majority of the human species is, it is a matter of ridding your body and mind of the things that kept it entrenched in the rings to begin with. It is a matter of learning how to listen and creating the ideal vessel from which to "hear." This may be looked at from the viewpoint of your individual life or from a larger perspective, as mankind on a time line, generation after generation, slowly gravitating outward until there is an awakening and expansion of consciousness and one is able to make their way back to the center. This is the natural progression within each one of us, hearing the call, knowing intuitively it is within and seeking reconnection with the source.

The gravitation outward did not happen in one or two generations and neither will the return to the center. This is because whichever ring you are currently at, you are only able to see (understand and recognize as truth) the ring immediately next to you. For example: A person who consumes the Standard American Diet (SAD) may become a vegetarian (consuming no animal flesh), a vegetarian may become a vegan (consuming no animal products) and a vegan may become a raw and living foodist (consuming only plant matter in its natural form). There are exceptions, but usually we are only able to grasp and integrate an awareness that is just above the one we currently hold.

What would take us so far from home? Why would we venture into the outer rings when there is so much suffering there? Some say it is for the experience, that it is our choice. I do not argue that we choose everything we experience, our thoughts do create who we are and what we perceive. But why would we stay for so long, generation after generation, lifetime after lifetime, experiencing the same suffering? Why is it, when we recognize that we, and others, are suffering and no longer wish to live in such an unnatural way, we are unable to find the center again? Why is it that despite our seeking, we are still unable to find the source within ourselves to transform us and the planet into the world we envision?

We understand and perceive ourselves and the world around us through our mental filters. Everything heard, read and seen is interpreted through your mind, using your past experiences and observations as a filter for understanding. Since this filter determines your understanding of yourself and the world around you, you are limited by the filter or "glasses" you wear. This is fine if the glasses are clear. But what if the glasses are fogged up, the filter clogged with sediment, impeding your understanding and perception? Since the glasses have been with you since birth (and with mankind for centuries), you can't tell if anything is wrong—because you think your glasses are normal. What if our very bodies and minds have been so filled with sediment and toxins from living for generations in unnatural ways that we were no longer able to feel our way home, no longer able to sense what it is we need to do to return to the center? If everyone had the same sediment clogging their filters, the planet's civilizations would evolve much differently than if the glasses had been clear. How would our filters become clogged? What makes us unable to live in accordance with our soul? What would take us so far from home? What would cause such an imbalance within our bodies and minds that the planet would go so far awry?

Let's look at an example from nature: Consider a community of animals in their natural habitat, a community that civilization had not touched, such as a colony of chimpanzees. If you observed them, you would find a perfectly balanced structure has evolved. Harmony and natural law preside. Their existence is in balance with their environment, in balance with nature. A wonderful continuum of life exists between the planet, animal, plant, and microscopic life, all fulfilling their natural mode of existence, all dependent on one another and functioning in accordance with nature.

Imagine, if you will, something unnatural to the laws of nature being presented into this setting. Perhaps man destroys the natural food source and replaces it with trays of unnatural food. Out of necessity, the chimpanzees discontinue their natural diet and consume largely this unnatural diet that had been introduced into their environment. Soon, this unnatural food would cause illness in the bodies of the chimpanzees because they would be consuming food they were not designed to digest. Their organs would deteriorate under the continual stress. Disease would result. They would become weaker as a race. After subsequent generations, their appearance would change as their bodies compensated and tried to maintain health despite the onslaught of unnatural food. Their life spans would decrease dramatically. Since their very cells are now being created from food that is not natural to their bodies, their bodily chemistry would change. Emotions would be out of balance. Mental processes would become irrational. Social behavior would deteriorate and chaos would ensue. Each generation would be farther removed from what was once the natural, harmonious, pristine way of life enjoyed by their ancestors. Succeeding generations would not even know what their natural diet was and would take the current state of existence as normal, never knowing anything else.

Our race is not that different from that colony of chimpanzees. We share this environment with the other creatures and life forms native to earth. There is a delicate balance among all life on earth, just as in the chimpanzee colony. Basic biology teaches us that the chain of life functions in accordance with the laws of nature. The food chain is a continuum stretching from the smallest microbes to the largest creatures inhabiting our planet. The ninety-two (plus) minerals and trace elements found in our bodies are first found in the earth. These elements continually transform as they follow the continuum of life down through the food chain and back into the earth to again spring forth and support life. It is not a stretch to understand that when this natural food chain is disrupted (the very molecular structure altered and then reintroduced into the chain again) there would be disharmony in the environment and imbalance in the life forms through which it passes.

In other aspects, we are unlike the chimpanzees in my example. Because we possess higher intelligence and the ability to reason, we have used these attributes to adapt to the chaos of our civilization. Because we perceive ourselves as separate from everyone else, we have invented weapons to defend ourselves. First, these weapons defended and destroyed on an individual level, now they defend and destroy on a planetary scale. We have fashioned a medical mentality that "cures" our illnesses through suppression of symptoms, ignoring the root cause. We ingest man-made poisons and call it medicine, not understanding we are insuring our extinction in the process. We have used our laboratories to further corrupt our food supply, in an attempt to make it "better," not realizing "better" can only be obtained through noninterference with nature's law. We have created various religions and superstitions in an attempt to explain and control what is unknown to us. None of these Band-aids would be necessary in a civilization whose inhabitants were not cut off from experiencing their source directly.

The toxic state our bodies are in from the unnatural diet we consume and the unnatural way we live prevents us from recognizing what is truth. We are not able to feel the center within our bodies because our energy centers have been blocked and our intuitive abilities concealed due to the sediment blocking our filters. The state of our bodies and minds has shaped our thoughts, beliefs, attitudes and behavior. What is perfectly natural, what is *nature's law,* has been obscured and deleted from our range of perception. This is why so many seek but few find. The evolutionary pull is alive in all of us and those who are seeking are answering the call, yet the direct experience they desire eludes them because they are unknowingly living in ways that keep their filters clogged.

The gravitation outward, away from the center, occurs on an individual and collective level. Anything that is not natural, anything that is not in harmony with nature, takes you away from the center. Since the physical body is the extension of the spirit, anything detrimental that is done to the physical body naturally takes you away from your true self. The ingestion of unnatural substances creates a varying energy vibration within the body explained organically as illness and disease. This literally changes the frequency in which your cells vibrate, making it impossible to align with the center. While in this misalignment (toxic state), you are unable to use your natural intuitive ability of *direct knowing* and thus, you cannot feel within you what is needed for your realignment. This change in frequency, this separation from the center, sets the foundation for myriad negative feelings, uneasiness and mental anguish that is the root of the suffering we inflict upon ourselves and each other. As these perpetuate, energy blocks are created within the energy field and your Chakra System, further separating us from the direct experience of the center. In turn, these negative feelings and inner conflicts are manifested through our outward attitudes and actions and are reflected in the world we see around us.

The area that has taken us furthest from the center is our diet. The relation between the food we eat and our body goes far beyond anything we have learned about nutrition. There is no part of your being that your food does not affect. This is because food is not only fuel, it is the direct infusion of your environment into your physical being. This infusion naturally sends the necessary nutrients to the systems of the body, but it also feeds the soul. Ingesting a diet that is in balance with nature is necessary to bring your physical and mental bodies into alignment with your soul. In changing what we put into our bodies to what is natural and life-giving, we transform the energy that makes up our physical body and open ourselves to feel and know what is beyond our grasp at our current state of awareness. Through this transformation, our filters are purified, our glasses cleared and our ability to perceive our center is enhanced. The mental and emotional hindrances will take care of themselves as we experience who we truly are *directly*. Mental suffering and conflict arise out of the absence of this knowing and mental suffering subsides with the alignment of mind, body and spirit.

Through the purification of your body comes emotional and mental release. Each release will take you to the next level in which you will be better able to directly perceive what you need to expedite your return home. The changes you experience will lead you to further growth and expansion of awareness. Because you have been conditioned since birth to fit into the current societal structure and belief system, you will need to recognize your self-limiting beliefs and the ways in which your thoughts create toxins within your body and energy field. These negative thoughts are perpetuated in a vicious cycle by the unnatural diet being consumed and also serve to keep your filter "clogged."

The residue of our living in a state of misalignment from our soul will not vanish overnight. The issues that have developed because of our separation need to be understood and released. The self-imposed limitations that keep us in the outer rings, such as fear, low self-esteem, negative self-image, lack of confidence and the belief in our autonomy can be changed with a thought. The process of cleansing these blockages is a natural one. In opening yourself to feel the unity of all life through purification of your body, you will be breaking the cycle that has held you there. In breaking the cycle, you can be restored to your natural state, one of radiant health, abundant energy, clarity of mind and great inner peace.

Divine Diet

I HAVE DEDICATED AN ENTIRE chapter to the subject of diet because our diet is one of the most overlooked and misunderstood aspects of our being. I cannot emphasize enough the importance of making dietary changes to enhance your spiritual experience.

Prior to the Kundalini activation, I had what I considered to be a "healthy" diet and lifestyle. I had been vegetarian for about five years, a decision my husband and I made overnight after reading *Diet for A New America*, by John Robbins. Meat is among the densest of foods, carrying a heavy energetic vibration. The elimination of meat from your diet will improve not only your health, but your mental outlook as well. When we consume the flesh of dead animals, we are ingesting the suffering of that animal. As the animal is led to slaughter, they sense that death is imminent. They smell the blood and hear the pain of the animals who preceded them. As this happens, their primal survival instincts kick in. They release adrenaline and other hormonal substances born of this terror, which quickly spread throughout their bodies. These substances (and the energy from their terror) are locked in the flesh, which we then consume, making it part of us. When you discover the connection within yourself to all of life, you will understand that all life is sacred. All life is a part of you and a part of God. To kill another sentient life, with such disregard for its existence, especially when there is no need to do so, carries heavy karmic implications for our souls. The suffering we inflict on our fellow creatures serves to keep us in this karmic wheel, until we understand the implications of our actions and change them.

Part of my transformation facilitated by the activated Kundalini energy has included not only my emotional cleansing but a physical cleansing, which in turn cleared the way for further expansion of consciousness and energetic experiences. I became interested in improving my diet and bought a juicer. Included with my juicer was a tape by Jay "The Juiceman" Kordich. He described himself as a raw-foodist, someone who consumes only raw, uncooked plant food, still in its natural state. At first this seemed strange to me. How could you not cook your food? Still, as I listened to the tape I could not ignore the truth I was hearing: "Life comes from life and death comes from death; cooked food is dead, the life-giving nutrients and life force have been killed; you cannot nourish your body on dead food; we are the only species on the planet who alters its food before consuming it." The energy started beating wildly in my chest (that familiar signal from my soul telling me I'm on the right track) and I was consumed with finding out more about this lifestyle. As I searched the Internet, I found a whole community of people who follow this lifestyle, as well as many books and Web sites offering support, advice and information. (See the Living and Raw Food Resources section.)

I immediately began to replace the vegetarian cooked foods I was eating with a raw vegetarian diet. I was driven by this inner knowing that this is what I must do to achieve a deeper level of connection with the Divine Source that I felt flowing through me. I knew this was my next step. The incredible transformation that followed surpassed anything I had imagined or expected. This is something that you cannot possibly understand until you experience it for yourself. The results were immediate. My body just took over. Toxins were eliminated, my energy soared, I needed much less sleep and I lost all excess weight. Best of all, I felt a dramatic deepening of the Divine connection within me as the filters of my body and mind were cleared. My mind became incredibly calm and peaceful and meditation was a breeze. I was able to intuit during my readings with greater clarity, getting more accurate, detailed information with a lesser degree of focusing. I had no idea of the difference diet would make until I experienced it directly. I had no idea that I wasn't functioning optimally until I experienced a higher state of awareness facilitated by consuming food in its natural state.

I realize that the concept of eating exclusively raw, uncooked plant food is quite a stretch for most of society, still deeply entrenched in the practices of consuming enormous amounts of animal products, processed, convenience and junk foods. These practices have taken us so far from our origins that we are unable to feel our inner guidance. We have strayed so far from what is natural that we no longer are able to understand what should be as apparent as the sun and the moon.

When I first heard about raw and living foods, it touched me to the core of my being. I instantly *knew* this was truth and I was shocked that something so simple and self-evident had never been questioned. The following words, spoken by Jesus and quoted from *The Essene Gospel of Peace,* gives us these basic truths—truths, that if followed, will change the nature of our very physiology, transforming our consciousness and allowing us to experience our divinity directly. *But I say unto you: Kill neither men, nor beasts, nor yet the food which goes into your mouth. For if you eat living food, the same will quicken you, but if you kill your food, the dead food will kill you also. For life comes only from life, and from death comes always death. For everything which kills your foods, kills your bodies also. And everything which kills your bodies kills your souls also. And your bodies become what your foods are, even as your spirits, likewise, become what your thoughts are. Therefore, eat not anything which fire, or frost, or water has de-*

stroyed. For burned, frozen and rotted foods will burn, freeze and rot your body also. — Jesus, The Essene Gospel of Peace.

A natural diet of fruits and vegetables was the original plan for our species as described in the first book of the Bible, *And God said, 'Behold, I have given you every herb bearing seed, which is upon the face of all the earth, and every tree, in which is the fruit of a tree yielding seed; to you they shall be for meat'* (Genesis 1:29).

I have found that as people move along on a spiritual path they naturally gravitate toward a "lighter diet" (a diet of lighter vibration). A meat eater may stop eating red meat and later may become vegetarian by abstaining from fowl and fish. As he grows in spiritual understanding and feels the deepening within his being, he may continue toward a lighter diet and stop the intake of all animal products. Later, as he further transforms his consciousness, a diet of exclusively raw and living foods may be adopted. These changes are not for the faint of heart. It takes great commitment and courage to break out of the existing level of awareness and greater commitment to maintain positive change amidst a society whose values and beliefs serve to keep us in the experience of separation.

As you begin to purify your diet, your bodies (physical, mental, spiritual) will begin to detoxify. On the physical level, common detoxification symptoms include: headaches, chills, fever, aches, pains, diarrhea, constipation and rashes. When you begin consuming food that is natural to your body, it can stop dealing with the onslaught of unnatural foods and energy is then freed up for detoxification. Your body begins "house-cleaning."

Throughout your life, toxins have been accumulating in your body. These are toxins in the form of pollution, chemicals, pesticides, preservatives and residues from cooked food that the body was unable to assimilate and dispose of. Through the accumulation of these toxins, the body becomes less efficient in dealing with them and the tissues and organs become saturated, bogged down and cease to function optimally. This condition is known as toxemia, and is the basis for all physical illness and disease. It is the reason our bodies degenerate as we age.

During detoxification, toxins that have been stored in your tissues, fat cells, bones and organs are dumped into your bloodstream for elimination. You experience unpleasant physical symptoms (which we have come to perceive as illness) as your body works to rid itself of these substances. Many people abandon their improved diet at this point, mistakenly thinking the new diet is making them sick, instead of understanding the body's natural healing abilities are at work.

Physical detoxification is the easy part. As you continue to detoxify at the physical level, your etheric bodies also detoxify. These are your energy blocks, past experiences, thoughts, perceptions and beliefs that have been held within your energy field by the density of your physical body. This is when your "issues" come to the surface. All the things you have shoved aside and hid from view will come to the forefront. The feelings you have repressed and refused to feel will erupt, demanding attention. You may experience mood swings, grouchiness, anger, fear, confusion and emotional pain. Layers of blockages are being brought to the surface to be released. As each layer surfaces, you will experience the emotion associated with the block. This can be something from this lifetime or a past lifetime. Eventually, all layers need to be released for you to experience the inner peace of direct communion with the Divine.

To understand how diet can have such a dramatic effect in all aspects of your life you must first understand that food is energy. This energy is the same "stuff" that flows through the physical body, the planet, the universe and beyond. The energy that is taken into your body is also given out by your body. The vibrations you take in, you give out. If the food taken into the body is of pure vibration, that is, close to its natural state, unaltered, it is able to meld with the body, creating an aura that resonates with the natural state of your spirit, your soul. There is no separation between the spirit and body. You *are* conscious energy. What you do to your physical body directly affects your spirit or soul. Neither is there a separation between your body and mind. How you feel about what you eat and what you think of as nourishing to your body can cause either conflict or harmony.

Food affects mood, mood is thought, thoughts dictate the energy you give out around you (positive or negative). When food is ingested, this energy is then part of the physical aware-ness that you now occupy (the food becomes part of what comprises your body, therefore, your mind). Food is a con-nection for the physical body to the rest of creation. When this energy (food) that is taken in is pure, it brings with it more of the "stuff" you are made of; thus, you feel "closer to God," "clear and peaceful" and you feel a sense of well-being. You are literally vibrating at a rate that is in alignment with the Source. On the other hand, if the food you consume is not natural, not in balance with nature, your body cannot main-tain its pure vibration, imbalance results, disease ensues and your mental clarity and thought processes no longer resonate with your soul's energetic vibration. Your glasses have become foggy and you can no longer feel or sense your true essence through the vehicle of your physical body. This is what has happened to most people on our planet. The repercussions of this disharmony are being felt on a planetary scale as well as in each of our lives.

There has been scientific research regarding the concept of "food affecting mood" and there have been many docu-mented correlations found. However, this research assumes that food is "other than" the physical body and it observes these correlations from a scientific standpoint, a very one-sided observation. The whole picture cannot be understood with our intellect, nor explained through solely scientific means, because our minds and our physical bodies are only a part of who we are. This has been the limitation of scientific study since the beginning of time.

Since the food you consume is pure energy, it melds with your own energy and dictates the energy you give out. Say your diet consists of potato chips, chocolate cake, refined and processed foods. You may think positive thoughts and perceive yourself as a spiritual person, feel peaceful and even experience some transcendental states. This is all relative. When the vibration of the energy (food) you take into your body has been altered from its natural state, *you are altered from your natural state.* It can be no other way. You are only able to think positive thoughts and uplift your perceptions to a certain degree; to the degree that the foods (energy) you take in allow. You will not know there is an even "higher" way to feel until you experience it. The more you eat food in its pure, raw form, the further you purify your body and transform your energy (vibration) to align with the Source.

You cannot separate your mental body from your physical body when considering what food to eat. Many people eat for emotional reasons, reacting to their mental state and trying to feel better through the indulgence of unhealthful food, as if their bodies were separate from their minds, as if they could feed their emotions directly, without feeling the effects within their body.

Everything is affected by your food choices. How you *feel* about your food choices immediately and directly affects your mood and attitude. This is because you directly feel the effects of what you eat within your body. When you feel bad about what you eat, either mentally or physically, you send those messages throughout your being; this in turn affects your energy vibration, creating a downward spiral. You continue to eat in this detrimental way, even though you know you shouldn't. You are, in essence, eating at an energetic vibrational level to match the current vibrational level of your physical body. If you eat at a purer, higher vibrational level (whole, natural foods diet), your mood is similarly affected and you feel good about yourself, which is perpetuated by how good you feel physically, which is, of course, expressed in your attitude and thoughts about yourself, which is manifested in your outward actions, and so on.

Your spirit reflects what the other two bodies are sending it. If you are eating in a way that creates a denser energy within your physical body (heavy foods such as animal products, heavily processed foods, junk foods, etc.), your mentality and thoughts reflect these choices and you suffer from the subsequent separation from your spiritual center. You experience conflict, anxiety, stress, and/or illness as your spirit tries to get your attention and bring you back, closer to your true nature, back into alignment. Because our glasses are foggy, our filters clogged, we don't recognize these signals for what they are and continue through our lives without the peace and vibrant health that is our birthright.

A change to a pure, raw, vegetarian diet will serve to alter your body's chemistry (or vibration) as you align more and more with the planet. When you eat, you are placing into your body elements that will dictate how it functions (vibrates). These elements (food) affect your other bodies (mind, spirit) as well. None is autonomous. As you eat natural, unaltered food, you experience a feeling of peace and well-being. This is simply a lightening of your vibration as your cells literally expand with lighter, finer energy.

You have heard the cliche "you are what you eat." It can also be said that "you experience what you eat." The cells and tissues of your body are only as good as the fuel (energy) you have taken in for their formation. Your level of perception, awareness and physical experience of the energy of creation through your physical body can only expand to the level of the energy vibration (food) you have used to create the body which you perceive through.

When the body is being nourished with pure food, energy is aligned and the conscious energy that you are is melded to everything else. There is less of a perception of yourself being "separate" because the very energy that makes up your body has changed and you feel more like "everything else."

This explains the feeling of peace and well-being that is experienced with a raw and living food diet. It is so simple. The perception of separation is more easily changed when your physical body is more in tune with the universe. To bring your physical body more in tune with the universe, simply bring food (vital energy) into your physical body that is in tune with the universe. That means food as provided by nature, in its natural state.

These changes did not come easily for me. I have swayed back and forth between a vegetarian and vegan diet and later, between a vegan and raw/living foods diet as I dealt with my issues and learned to be at peace in this physical world. As my body lightened, my awareness increased. As my awareness increased, my perceptions expanded. Through this process, I have come to the realization that we cannot enjoy total communion with the Divine while in the physical body, without preparing our vessel for the joining. The area of diet is one that we have complete control over. Adopting a pure, vegetarian, natural foods diet is the most powerful catalyst for spiritual growth that I know of. It sets in motion a process of spiritual unfoldment as your body is literally transformed and higher states of consciousness are experienced. All other practices take us just to the edge of what is possible. I have included many excellent books in the Raw and Living Food Resources Section for those who are ready to purify their Divine vessel and accelerate their spiritual transformation.

CHAPTER 17

Finding the Quiet Within

W<small>HY DO WE NEED TO FIND</small> the quiet within? I used to wonder that myself. I wondered about the whole concept of this world that existed "within." My world existed around me, *outside* of me. It consisted of the things that happened to me and the people I interacted with. It never occurred to me that I could stop these things, even momentarily, and focus on something else. As I went through my life, being affected by all that was around me, I felt out of control. I *was* out of control. I didn't know I could change the way I reacted to situations, or the way I perceived people. I didn't understand what it meant to "go within." The stress I constantly created for myself kept my focus on the external. It was not until these things became overwhelming and affected my health that I began to seek out this world that lies within. Those things that are our stressors can actually help us go within. They are yet another catalyst for change.

Stress can be defined as the absence of relaxation, both physical and mental. When you are in a state of stress, your body contracts and closes up. You are not open to receive Divine guidance. You are not open enough to hear the voice that is your conscience. When you are under stress, you are fighting against the good things that are waiting to come to you. You are not open to recognize, notice or receive them. In addition, you stop *creating* them through your thoughts, instead, focusing only on the situation that you are perceiving as stressful. The thoughts that produce stress are negative, which lowers your energy level and your vibration. They are critical thoughts, thoughts of not being good enough and of not accomplishing enough. They are thoughts of expecting the worst from the world around you. When you have these types of thoughts, they materialize. This sets up a vicious cycle, because the more you focus on your stress and the more you have these negative thoughts, you create more of the same. What you focus on expands.

On the other hand, when you are in a state of relaxation, your mind is open to new ideas and your heart is open to give and receive love. You can draw to yourself the good things you want and create them through your thoughts. The thoughts that accompany relaxation are positive thoughts, thoughts of abundance, of happiness, of trust and love. They are thoughts that expect the world to be a positive place. These thoughts also perpetuate themselves. Again, what you think, you create. What you create, you experience.

To connect with your Divine guidance you must find that quiet place within. That means you have to learn to slow down your mind. You have to stop the constant racing and worrying that is so much a part of our society. We are always rushing to the next thing. We seem to thrive on turbulence and are in perpetual motion. We consider idleness a sign of laziness. We do not recognize that if we allow ourselves time for relaxation, we will actually be more productive. When our minds are clear, we can concentrate. When we have mental clarity, we can see our purpose and accomplish more.

Stress is something I have an intimate knowledge of. Earlier in this book I referred to myself as a "stress ball." This description certainly fit me up until a few years ago. I was constantly worrying about something, anything. If things were going well, I worried something would go wrong. My mind would race continually. I worried about what people thought of me. I worried I would forget something I was supposed to do. I worried about my makeup, my clothes, my car, my job and my future. Whenever I did something, I thought of the next three things I needed to do. There was always one more thing to do. I was never happy. People around me were always telling me to lighten up, but I literally didn't know how. I was acting the way I always had, the only way I knew. I felt they were right, but I didn't know how to change. I tried to relax and slow down but I didn't know how. I thought it was futile. I also found it difficult to change my thought patterns that had produced my stress in the first place. I was creating more stress as I tried to learn to relax!

When I developed TMJ syndrome, and my lower jaw literally locked in the closed position I knew something had to change. This was my wake-up call. It really jolted me into action when I realized how harmful my constant stress had been to my body. I want to make something clear. When I talk about my constant stress, I don't mean that I had such a hard life, or unbearable circumstances. I was no different from the rest of middle-class America. I had a husband, two kids, a full-time job and house payment. Rather, I *created* it for myself. I produced my stress, as we all do. I was the one who perceived everything to be so stressful. I put the demands and expectations on myself. I was the one who was unable to be still and quiet for five minutes without feeling uncomfortable. Of course, I didn't understand all that at the time. As with most of us, I was stuck in my "cycle," muddling through life, reacting to events with no purpose or direction.

I was determined to find a way to reduce my stress. I got some books on yoga and meditation. I had heard meditation could help. I began taking yoga classes and began to practice my meditation daily. Boy, did I have a long way to go! I approached meditation as I did everything, by making it a struggle. I tried to force my mind to stay quiet. I tried to force my mental focus and when my mind would stray, I became frustrated and impatient. Yet, something wonderful was happening. I found that during the time when I was at yoga class, under the instruction of the teacher, I was able to make my mind and body be *still*. I learned what it felt like to turn my focus *inward*. I remember how wonderful it felt to achieve that state of relaxation. I learned that to meditate really required no specific method. There is no right way or wrong way to meditate. Basically, it is only the quieting of the mind and the blocking out of all the external things. Whatever method works best for you is what you should do. Everyone needs to experiment to find what works for them. (Meditation is discussed at length in Chapter 19.)

I continued my meditation practice and gradually found I could quiet my mind for longer periods of time. This was not easy for me. My mind would wander and I would continually have to bring it back. Some days were easier than others and it was still some time before I learned to carry this stillness and relaxation over into other parts of my life. But, I was making progress. I now understood the connection between my mental state and my physical body. I understood that when I quieted my mind, my body followed, and vice versa. These days my mind is quiet and calm. It functions in a state of stillness and I focus it on a moment by moment basis, without pushing it onto the next thought, or lingering on a past thought. I have learned to monitor my thoughts and can quickly change a negative thought to a positive one before it can "catch hold." This is the greatest gift I have ever given myself. All that has happened to me, my spiritual growth, my self-understanding, the activation of the Kundalini and the merging into higher consciousness came out of my first learning how to go within.

Those things that hold our attention on the external are sometimes serving a purpose. I now know that I spent so many years trying to keep my mind busy in an attempt to keep it from thinking about the things that were painful to me. I have already discussed my childhood and those painful issues that I ultimately dealt with. Each time I became quiet and tried to relax, I was reminded of those painful things that I was unable to deal with and I would again rush to occupy my mind.

Illness can be a catalyst too, as my bout with TMJ had been. It took my body having a severe reaction to the stress I was inflicting on it to get my attention and to prompt me into making a change. As you begin to focus on that which lies within, you may find your issues coming to the surface. They will beg for attention now that you are listening. This is a wake-up call for you. These issues have been holding you back, keeping you from realizing your full potential. Now is the time to work through them, to learn their lessons. If you look deep enough, you will find you already have what you need to resolve them.

Take a mental journey now. Go back in time, to when you were a child. Try to remember what you thought about. Did you daydream? What did you dream of doing? What did you enjoy? What brought you happiness and joy? Is there something you always wanted to do but haven't done? Is there a hobby you have not pursued? Go back to that time before your thoughts were shaped by society's messages. Go back to that innocence. Go back to that center of your being. There you will find your true self. Your soul is waiting there.

CHAPTER 18

Loving Yourself

ONE OF THE MOST IMPORTANT THINGS you can do for your spiritual evolution is to love yourself. After that, everything else will fall into place. When you love yourself, perceived faults and all, you are then able to love others, perceived faults and all. You will not know inner peace until you unconditionally love and accept yourself. The conflict you see played out all around you and throughout the world stems from the conflict each one feels within themselves. You will find it easy to make positive changes in your life (healthier diet, nurturing relationships, right livelihood) when you love yourself, because you will naturally gravitate toward what is good for you. When you love yourself, you value yourself and therefore you take care of yourself. In short, you will stop putting up roadblocks to your success and happiness. You will be able to hear the voice within guiding you and you will naturally come into alignment with your soul.

Sounds simplistic? It is. What you are is pure love. Any thought that takes you away from that takes you away from your true self. Your inner voice—your soul—yearns to express itself fully. By giving yourself love and acceptance you will be allowing this voice to be heard. It may not always take you in the direction you have been going and it may not fit anything you have expected, but, if followed, it will always lead you home.

141

I want you to notice I did not say you need to *learn* to love yourself. There are many psychiatrists and therapists making a living trying to teach us to love ourselves. What you need to do is simply to love yourself. Nothing is required but your willingness to let go of the past. Right now, in this moment, no matter what you think you need to work on, no matter how much weight you want to lose, no matter how badly you feel about your past deeds, no matter what you haven't accomplished, simply stop all this mental chatter and embrace yourself, totally.

I know this is a foreign concept to many in our society. We have become addicted to self-help techniques and the constant striving for what is better. We hold a picture of ourselves that is just out of reach, while we "work on" our faults, waiting for a better "us" to emerge. This mind-set keeps us in a constant state of dissatisfaction with ourselves. Our focus is on what we lack, rather than what we already are. If we fall back in our efforts, we often give up, disgusted with ourselves for our failure and use this as "proof" of our unworthiness.

What is necessary is to change the way you perceive worthiness. Everyone, without exception and regardless of stature or deeds is infinitely worthy, totally whole and not lacking in any way. That is the truth of your being but it is not the truth of the reality of the world we have created. Strip away all the conditioning. Understand that you are not defined by any accomplishment, by any educational degree, by any profession, by any income bracket, by any dollar figure in your savings account, by any societal status, by any treatment you received as a child or by anyone's opinion or view of you. Most importantly, understand you are not defined by your limitations. Strip away all that society has used to place value on you and see yourself for what you truly are. When you stop measuring yourself by society's standards, it is much easier to embrace your true self.

The stress that is rampant in our society is a result of our constant striving to live up to all these expectations, so we will be "worthy." To grow spiritually, we need to give up what no longer works for us and, in many cases, that requires the courage to realize we have been wrong in the way we were living our life. Rather than blaming ourselves for our "ignorance," we can simply realize that because of our new awareness, what previously felt right no longer fits. This is as it should be. We are constantly changing but are often reluctant to let go of beliefs and practices that no longer serve us.

We are in these physical bodies for the expression and experience of our own divinity. It is through these physical bodies (and our everyday lives) that we will come to know the Divine Source that we are. The love and acceptance you give yourself, you give to others automatically. Do not allow your perceptions of limitation or faults keep you from recognizing what you are now, in this moment. Always present, in each moment, is the opportunity for full expression of your soul. This expression is wonderfully unique, as the Divine Source is represented through your unique physical and mental bodies. Total acceptance of your human frailties (and everyone else's) allows you to experience the presence of this divinity within you and to see it in others.

I have found that always, without exception, as the conditioned thoughts arise, they take me farther away from the direct experience of the divinity within. When I slip back into the habit of self-critical thinking and negative self-talk, I instantly notice the absence of the Kundalini energy that normally flows through my body, as the negative thoughts lower my physical vibration so it is no longer compatible with the Divine energy. My energy centers close and I am unable to feel the connection to the Divine Source. The connection is still there, but my vibration becomes denser through the negative thoughts, altering my ability to perceive the source. Who and what I am does not change, only my perception (my thoughts) of who I am changes and therefore my experience changes. Not surprisingly, once my experience changes, so does the outward manifestation (my attitudes and behavior) of my inner experience. Soon, I am in conflict with my kids and those around me and I find myself focusing on the hopelessness of the world's problems. This escalation happens in a matter of minutes. By simply noticing the self-limiting and self-defeating mental chatter and releasing those thoughts, I once again find myself filled with the Divine energy and instantly my outward manifestation reflects my inner experience.

The energy that we are is conscious of itself and responds in whatever way we direct. Therefore, it is not that the Divine energy withdraws if my thoughts are not loving, then returns when I relinquish the negative thoughts; rather, my physical experience of the energy being absent is merely my choosing (by my negative thoughts) to have an experience of negativity toward myself. This experience takes me "farther" from my true self and in that "distance" there is the experience of separation or, the experience of the absence of the Divine Source. This experience of separation is where most people now reside, and it is the root cause of our suffering.

For me, it has been easy to track the responses of this Divine energy in relation to my thoughts and moods. It has been painfully obvious when I am not in alignment with my true self and has been equally obvious when I release my conditioned thoughts and responses and let the energy direct me. These unseen energetic phenomena are happening to everyone, at all times. You are this energy, you are directing the energy with your thoughts and you are experiencing the reality you have created. One of the most important things you can do to become consciously aware of this energy within you and therefore to accelerate your spiritual growth, is to stop all striving and judgment and completely love yourself exactly as you are. In this acceptance there is surrender and in surrender there is revelation.

Nothing is stopping you from total acceptance and peace within yourself at this moment. If you are willing, and truly wish to, you can do so. Open to yourself, send love inward, draw it to yourself and you will soon find it overflowing.

CHAPTER 19

Meditation

THE SINGLE MOST IMPORTANT THING you can do for your spiritual growth is to meditate. I cannot stress this enough. Through meditation we learn what it feels like to be pure consciousness, without the limitations of the mind. Through meditation we learn to turn off the mind chatter and hear our inner voice.

When we meditate, we are actually altering our brain wave patterns. We are expanding the ways in which we can perceive things. I believe the brain actually reconfigures itself to allow for this new type of communication. This new perception is the untapped sixth sense we have, the ability to tap into infinite knowledge. Meditation lets us exercise and develop that ability.

When you begin meditation, it can seem difficult, even impossible. That is because you are trying to use an ability that has never been accessed and it has atrophied. With practice, you build up this ability, like an unused muscle, until it reaches its full potential. It keeps getting easier and soon it is a muscle that begs for use if ignored.

In meeting with clients, I hear the same thing over and over, "I know I need to meditate, I just don't have time." I know very well how life gets in the way, especially at first, if you perceive it as more of a struggle than something relaxing. However, if you are reading this book, you are well along on your spiritual path and you owe it to yourself to commit to a meditation practice. Remember that the very reason for your life is to grow spiritually, period! Nothing else that you perceive as important in your life is as important as that. Furthermore, once you are meditating regularly, you will reap such wonderful benefits, including a shift in your priorities, which will make the rest of your life fall into place.

The second most common thing I hear from my clients is, "I try to meditate, I just can't stop my thoughts." I know that feeling very well. Believe me, if I can learn to stop my thoughts, anyone can. My mind used to race a mile a minute. I always had to have one thing going and three things floating around. When I first began to meditate, the thoughts came on like gangbusters—the more I tried to quiet them, the more they came up. If there was ever a pause in my brain activity, I would panic, it was so foreign to me. Many times I felt like quitting. Many times I did. Eventually, my search for answers won out and I instinctively turned inward, finding a method that worked for me.

There is no right way to meditate. This is a very individual thing. When working with clients who are having difficulty, I advise them to do the following: Sit in a comfortable position. I like a straight-backed chair with arms. You may sit on the floor, lotus-style if you like. It really doesn't matter, as long as you are comfortable. It is also important for your back to be straight. This allows for the free flow of energy up through your Chakra System. If I am slumping, I can actually feel the build up of energy in my heart center and it gets very uncomfortable. When you are comfortable, take some deep breaths, through your nose. Exhale slowly and let your body relax with each exhale. Do not focus on your mind, do not worry about being absolutely quiet, just relax and enjoy being still. If you are having difficulty relaxing, continue this practice until you feel relaxed. It may take you several days to get past this stage; that's OK, you are unlearning a whole lifetime of ingrained patterns. Next, close your eyes and picture your mind as a closed fist, closed up tightly in a ball, contracted in thought. Then picture that fist opening slowly, just as your hand would if you were allowing the fist to open on its own. This open state is one of expansion. There may still be a few thoughts floating by. That's all right. Do not focus on them. Do not get upset or frustrated. Do not even consider them. When you have any thought about "stopping thoughts," you are only creating another thought! The trick is to open your mind (relax the fist) and release all control. Try to sit in this open space, without contracting the mind again. If you do not focus on the thoughts and merely allow them to float by at will, you are taking away their power over you. Please do not make this into work. It is really very effortless. It is simply resting in the source of your being. Cease all mental effort and just allow yourself to *be*.

At this point, you should not be meditating toward any goal. You should not be trying to focus on an object, or hold a single thought in your mind. These practices are good for learning mind control, but what we are trying to do is find the place of "no mind." This only happens in the place "between the thoughts." Some people like to listen to music while they meditate. This can be good to quiet your mind and relax your body, but the music keeps you focused on a sound coming from outside your body. In meditation we are trying to gain a perception of what's inside, not what's outside.

Once I understood why there was difficulty in stopping the thoughts, it made it easier for me and I no longer got frustrated. Your mind is your ego. Your ego is thought. Without thoughts, you have no ego. You exist as pure energy until the mind comes into play, creating a perception of who you are. When we try to stop the thoughts, we are killing the ego. To stop thinking is to give up our identity and the mind will avoid this at all costs. It will conger up all kinds of thoughts to avoid having a lapse in identity. Have you ever had a song playing over and over in your head when nothing else was on your mind? The mind has a mind of its own!

If you continue to meditate, you will experience your issues coming to the surface. This is an inevitable part of spiritual growth. For me, this was very obvious. I would settle into that place of "no-mind" and have difficulty staying there. I would feel as if I hit a wall. I would experience a sinking feeling, sort of like floating to another level and then wham! There was something blocking me from holding the expanse any longer. I was experiencing an energy block. Something had to be released before I could go any further. I would often experience this feeling if I had been emotionally upset about something or if it had been a few days since I had meditated. To release the block, I would continue to try and hold the meditative expanse, inviting the feelings that were held there. Sometimes, a good cry was all it took. Other times, I needed to work something out with someone in order to reach peace of mind, and afterwards I was able to hold the meditative state for an even longer period. As time has gone by, I find reaching that state keeps getting easier and easier. I can "drop down" to the place of no-mind almost instantly, which is what I do during an intuitive session. Three years ago I would never have believed that I could ever stop my thoughts at will. Now I do it for a living!

Make meditation part of your daily practice. I meditate twice a day, usually forty-five minutes to one hour in the morning and at bedtime for thirty to forty-five minutes. I also experience such energetic phenomena during the night that I usually end up meditating in the middle of the night to get back to sleep. Before an intuitive session, I usually spend several minutes clearing my mind and focusing on the client who I'm expecting. In the beginning, I could only meditate for five or ten minutes at a time. The extension has been a natural process. Some days I feel as though I never want to come out of meditation. Some days I go about my day feeling as though I never did come out! As you continue with a meditation practice, you will find your methods, perceptions and purposes for the practice changing. Allow your feelings to guide you.

If you can't manage to meditate twice a day, once a day is fine. Don't worry about how much time you spend or feel guilty if you miss a day or two. As you progress, you will experience changes and fluctuations in your practice and methods. This is normal. Remain open to whatever comes and above all, follow your inner feelings, they will lead you to what is best for you.

The meditation below will help in opening your heart center. This is a powerful meditation and if repeated daily will serve to bring up your "issues," allowing for healing and release. You must be prepared to do this emotional work if you want to unblock the center and allow your true self to flow through. As you direct love inward you will also be directing it outward.

The more you do this meditation, the more your outward perceptions will change. This is because you see the outside world as a mirror of yourself. When you totally accept and love yourself, you love and accept others and the illusion of separation begins to fade.

Meditation to Open the Heart Center

Sit in a relaxed position, in a chair or on the floor. You should have your back straight so the chakras are aligned along your spine and the energy can flow freely. You can take as long as you like to do this meditation, extending the focus on each issue as you feel the need to. Plan to spend at least five minutes each day. You can add it onto your existing meditation practice or use it by itself.

Begin by taking several deep breaths, breathe deeply, from the diaphragm and as you exhale, relax your entire body. When you feel relaxed, turn your attention to the area in the middle of your chest, this is your heart center, the fourth chakra. This focus should be relaxed and effortless, do not concentrate or force your attention, let it be directed there naturally.

Visualize a large emerald-green ball in this center, see it spinning (it spins to your right). As it spins it becomes brighter and larger. Continue this visualization as you mentally repeat the following statements, directing them toward your heart center:

I love you.

I forgive you for your past hurts.

I totally accept you, including all your imperfections and faults.

I give you permission to heal and to feel safe.

I love you absolutely.

We are one.

Creating Peace

As you become more spiritually aligned, you will notice many things changing. You may not be comfortable with the same friends. You may not like the same music. You may feel the need to change your career, your home, your lifestyle. These changing tastes are a natural part of your spiritual growth. You will be drawn toward new things that will facilitate your growth. The things that aren't working in your life will become painfully obvious and you will feel compelled to eliminate everything that does not feel conducive to your new awareness.

In Buddhist philosophy and practices the process of bringing your life into alignment with your spirituality is called the "Eightfold Path." They are: Right View; Right Thought; Right Speech; Right Action; Right Livelihood; Right Effort; Right Mindfulness; Right Contemplation. What is "right" in any one of these areas is different for everyone and varies at different times throughout your life. What may have felt fine before may now cause you to feel uneasy. As your awareness expands, your vibration increases. The old will naturally fall away to be replaced with the higher ideal.

We all want to experience inner peace. Unfortunately, inner peace is something that is unfamiliar to most people in our society today. Inner peace is not something that happens when your outside circumstances change. You must create inner peace. This can be referred to as "weeding your garden." You must pinpoint the things that are causing you disharmony and find a way to change them.

When your energy blocks are cleared and your body purified, you will be able to distinctly feel the vibration of certain things. In this way, I have been able to pinpoint immediately the effect something is having on my energy field and make the necessary changes. However, you do not need to be able to feel things this distinctly to pinpoint the sources of your disharmony. Most people are all too aware of these things; the job you dislike, the relative you haven't spoken to in years, the house payment that's too large, the extra weight you haven't been able to lose or the unresolved guilt you feel over a past deed. You are not powerless to make these changes. If it is your will to create inner peace in your life, you will find it within yourself to make the necessary changes.

To experience inner peace, you must create quiet for yourself. Since our daily lives are so hectic and are usually running at a frantic pace, you must purposefully change your habits to allow for quiet time. There simply is no other way. This is a foreign concept to many people. The minute they walk into a room, the TV is turned on, sometimes only for "noise." The minute they get in the car, the radio is turned on. When we shop, we are bombarded with music. When we eat, we read a magazine or watch TV. We are so accustomed to having some activity or sound holding our attention to the outside world, that most of us have no idea how to listen to our inner voices. When you consciously carve out a quiet space for yourself, you can begin to connect with what's inside.

The first step to creating inner peace is to regulate what you allow into your consciousness. Everything you see and hear becomes a part of your energy. This is because your reaction (your experience of it) is stored in your body's energy field. An example of this is a child who may get nightmares after watching a scary TV program. We comfort him and tell him it isn't real, thinking he is young and impressionable and he cannot tell the difference between reality and fiction. This isn't the reason he is affected so strongly. The subconscious does not differentiate between reality and fiction. Your conscious mind may know that something is only a movie, but as you watch it, you are drawn into experiencing it; it evokes emotions. This experience is recorded in your energy field, as if you did experience it. The difference between you and the child is that the child is still "open." His body's energy centers have not yet been blocked. Whereas, you have been desensitized to these things, your energy centers no longer allows you to experience the effects these images have on your soul/ spirit. This desensitization is what has allowed humanity to continue along its self-destructive path. We are no longer able to sense the damage we are doing to our spirits.

The next step to creating an inner peace for yourself is to look at your life and take care of the issues you have pushed aside. If you haven't spoken to your brother in five years because of a fight, you need to contact him. It isn't important what his reaction is. What does matter is that you tried. You made a true and loving effort to reach out to heal the rift. If you then feel you have done all you can do, you can feel at peace with the situation. This is important to understand. If there is any unfinished business in your life, you need to address it. The outcome needn't be perfect. If you are coming from a place of love and openness, you can do no harm in the effort. What this will do is release that issue, meaning, the associated energy blockage and negative vibration that accompanied it will be released. It is these unresolved issues that create our karma[8]. As you advance along your spiritual path, you will eliminate the negative karma of this and previous lifetimes, allowing for the continued evolution of your soul.

To live in alignment with your soul you need to heed your inner voice—always. When you go ahead with something, even though you have a feeling you shouldn't, you are creating disharmony within your energy field. The action is actually recorded at a vibration that is different from your Divine Source. These actions take us farther into the experience of separation. As this pattern is repeated, energy blocks begin to gather in the associated chakras, cutting you off from the experience of your soul.

A common blockage I see in my clients is that of the fifth chakra. This is the center of will and communication. It is located in the throat area, near the thyroid gland. When someone does not "speak their mind" and this becomes a pattern with them (i.e. ,holding in what they feel they need to or should say), the fifth chakra becomes blocked. I can see this blockage clairvoyantly as I look at them. It is very common for this type of blockage to manifest itself as a sore throat or thyroid disorder. With this type of person, there is usually a lifetime pattern that needs to be addressed. As they become aware of their conflict in this area, they can work through their inability to communicate and become secure in speaking what they feel. The associated physical illness usually disappears as the blockage is cleared and harmony is restored.

An important distinction to understand is that the emotional blockages in our bodies are not the result of doing something "wrong." It is not the action or inaction that causes the problem. It is the way you *feel* about it. For example, if you have been told by your doctor that you need to lower your cholesterol and therefore should not eat hamburgers and you order one anyway, while feeling guilty because you feel you really should have ordered a salad, it is your feelings about this action that cause the disharmony, not the action. (Please note, there is a negative karma associated with the eating of dead animals, which is addressed in Chapter 16.) If a law is broken intentionally, the repercussions of that action have a negative effect on your soul's energy field. You have created negative karma surrounding that situation. However, if you unknowingly break a law, it does not carry the same energetic/spiritual implications. Again, it is the way you feel about the action, not the action itself, that brings disharmony. When I don't heed my inner knowing, I am sorry every time. I immediately feel the energy in my heart center become denser and I feel less peaceful. It takes my opening to this energy and feeling the implications of the action to release the blockage.

The process of releasing your blockages will come naturally to you as you continue on your spiritual path. This process has been happening all your life, whether you have been aware of it or not. Those issues and situations that keep coming up for you to deal with, causing you to feel irritable and uneasy, are your energy blockages coming to the surface to be dealt with. To release them, you need not agonize over what the cause of the distress is. Often, we are unable to pinpoint it. When you recognize these feelings of uneasiness and disharmony, go into meditation and focus on your heart center (as explained in Chapter 19). Invite the feelings to come, opening yourself to experience whatever you have been avoiding by focusing on this center. Allow yourself to fully feel what comes through. Cry, scream, or do whatever it takes to get the feeling out. By allowing it to flow through, you will be releasing it. Sometimes, there is layer upon layer of these blockages. You may feel a lightness after a clearing session, only to again feel the same emotions emerge at a later time. This is a deeper layer of energy that has been allowed to surface. This is not for the faint of heart. It takes courage and commitment to face and experience the emotions of the issues you have been avoiding. Nothing is as bad as we imagine. It is only the fear of these feelings that gives them power over us. Once you allow yourself to feel them, you will find the real pain was in the avoidance of them.

To create peace, you must consciously align your actions with your inner truth. Allow your inner direction to guide you to make the changes you need to make. Don't be afraid to feel your emotions. Allow them to flow out of you. In this flowing, there is healing. Let the barriers, facades and defenses fall away and allow yourself the freedom to be genuine.

Something that is usually overlooked in our search is the part the physical body plays in our ability to experience inner peace. Chapter 14 details this connection and its place in your spiritual understanding. It bears repeating here that you can only experience a Divine connection and, therefore, inner peace, to the extent your vessel (body) will allow. You must feed your body the right food so the organs and other systems will not be overworked. When you eat, you should feel peaceful afterwards, even spiritually enhanced. You should not be able to feel the workings of your digestion. You should not have indigestion, constipation or a feeling of being stuffed. You should not feel tired or sleepy after you eat. These things are unnatural. They are the result of your body having to work too hard to process and throw off the substances that were consumed. You must put pure, natural, unaltered food into your body so it can function optimally and become the vessel in which you can experience your divinity.

Inner peace can be greatly enhanced if you surrender to the Divine Source that is guiding your life. Your soul has a purpose here. Your mind can get in the way. Most of us are guilty of overanalyzing everything, second guessing even the minutest details of our lives. This need to control everything provides a false sense of security. When you release your need to know, something miraculous happens—you find that you *do* know. Your intellect can actually hinder your spiritual growth by keeping you in your current known reality. You can only experience what lies beyond when you drop the safety net of your intellect and open to what you do not know. Allow it to happen, whatever it may be. Experience everything with the wonder of a child. Trust that everything you need is coming to you at exactly the right time . . . because it is. The struggle is only within your mind. Surrender the need to analyze and trust in your inner guidance; it is the only way home.

CHAPTER 21

Balancing Your Inner and Outer Worlds

THE PRACTICE OF LIVING from a spiritual place in today's world is not always easy. Before you go out into the world, you center yourself through meditation, arm yourself with positive affirmations, hold love within your heart and vow to remain in this "place" throughout your day. You arrive at work to find someone has taken your parking space, the computer has gone down for the week, the file clerk misfiled the day's folders and your paycheck will be two days late. Add to this your mother-in-law's upcoming visit, your son's birthday party, your spouse's bad mood and the increase in your car insurance and you find all your good intentions were for naught. You pick yourself up, dust yourself off and vow to begin anew tomorrow.

Sometimes it may seem as if the only way to live in a way that is conducive to your emerging spirituality is to chuck it all and take up life in a monastery. Since this is neither attractive nor practical for most of us, you will need to learn to balance the two worlds. Sometimes the scale tips too far one way or the other, but you can easily regain the balance if you are flexible and learn to recognize what is happening. Most importantly, you must be willing to make changes in your life. Growth is not possible without change.

Because everyone's life is different and everyone is at a different place on their path, not everyone will find their per-

157

fect balance in the same way. You will need to seek out what works best for you. To find your perfect balance, you must first recognize those areas that present the greatest challenge for you. Maybe, it's the lady in the corner office who always looks at you with that smug smile as you pass. Maybe it's your children, who fight constantly between themselves or give you cause for worry. Maybe it's your mother's attitude when you visit. Identify those things that send you spiraling downward. Recognize that these things are pushing your buttons and understand that you need to adjust the way you are looking at them. Your perceptions of these situations cause your negative emotional responses to them. Learn to view these situations as lessons for growth and examine each for its purpose. Try to find a different way of handling them that takes the emphasis off what you're feeling and focuses on how you can help and empower the other person. In this way, your ego will be less involved and you will be viewing the situation from a place of love, rather than a place of defense. It may be necessary to stand up for yourself for the first time. It may be necessary for you to let go of something that has been causing you grief. Realize these situations are not going to go away. They are part of life. The way you choose to handle them is the deciding factor in whether they will continue to push your buttons or not.

As I ventured out into the world after the initial Kundalini activation, those things that keep us from growing and keep us in negative thought patterns were painfully obvious. Many things I heard and saw around me that I used to consider a normal part of everyday life now felt like fingernails on a chalkboard to me. I understood this was my higher-self's way of keeping me on the path, by keeping me from falling back into the familiar patterns that keep us from raising our vibrations and evolving. The things that were not conducive to my increased energy vibration stood out like a sore thumb.

One of the first things I noticed was that I rarely read the newspaper anymore. The newspaper usually reports on negative events like crime, the depressed economy, disasters and the newest scandals of our politicians. I noticed that after reading about these events, I felt my energy level drain as my thoughts circled around the negativity and sadness in the world. We feel the need to keep up on current events and to keep abreast of all these negative things, yet they add nothing positive to our lives. On the contrary, they add thoughts of helplessness, despair, worry and doubt. We use the events in the news as small talk throughout our day as we meet with others. We discuss these events with them and by doing so, draw the negativity to us and further amplify it as we share these thoughts. I am not suggesting that you ban the news media from your life, just be aware of this perpetuating cycle and understand its effect on you.

The area of entertainment follows suit. Television programs, movies, magazines and computer games all teach us to focus on the external. They enforce the importance of material things and their advertising leads us to feel we are lacking. Through them, we are given a set of standards that represent the "accepted" way to live, the "right" things to own and the "perfect" way to look. These things shape the values of our society and give our children false ideas of what is important. Certainly, there are educational television programs, worthwhile magazines and tasteful movies, but it is up to us to ascertain what will aid in our growth and what will detract from it. It is up to you what you allow into your mind. Stop following the social norm out of habit and follow your natural instinct to seek out what is good for you.

Another area I found I had to examine were my social activities. When I visited with friends and family and listened to the conversations that I used to participate in, I found them increasingly negative and shallow. People love to complain, and to have an audience seems to bring out even more complaints. Topics of conversation usually focus on what is wrong in our lives. We revel in telling each other about our latest tragedies and upheavals. We trade stories about that rude checker at the grocery store, the repeated repairs on our cars, the fight with our ex-spouse, the cat's veterinary bills or our inability to lose weight. As we speak of all this negativity, we lower our energy vibration and draw more of the same to ourselves. These thoughts also preclude us from thinking of positive things and, therefore, keep us from drawing positive things to ourselves. Often, we cannot think of anything to say unless we are complaining about something that has happened to us. There are people who will be unwilling to break out of this habit. You need to understand that you may not be compatible with all your previous friends. Some people need to hold onto their negativity and are unwilling to break away from what feels comfortable to them.

When you find yourself in one of these familiar conversations, instead of chiming in out of habit, change the subject or try to turn the conversation toward a more positive outlook. For instance, if your friend is complaining about her ex-husband's insincerity, you might look at her and say "Isn't it wonderful you realized you were incompatible so you could both find happiness with other people?" You don't do yourself any favors by allowing your thoughts to be sucked down through their complaints. Nor do you do them any favors by allowing them to continue with their downward spiral. Realize that you have the ability to control what you say, what you hear and what you think.

As you go through your daily activities, try to look at things in a new way. When you have contact with others, look past the physical and focus instead on the soul within. Know they are part of you and you are part of them. If you view them critically or in a judgmental way, stop yourself. Being aware of these automatic thoughts is the first step to changing them. It is fine to recognize what you see. For instance, if you see a person who is dirty and unshaven, just realize that is what you see—that they are dirty and unshaven. Do not place a judgment along with that observation. Do not conclude they are lazy, poor or bad. Understand that they are doing the best they can with what they have right now. Who among us has not been down at one time or another? It is a rare person who has not experienced some form of depression, illness, unemployment, broken home, child abuse, violent behavior or drug and alcohol abuse. Our lives are a constant flow of ups and downs. Do not judge others because you are viewing them during one of their "downs."

I find the more I think about my spirituality, the easier it is to maintain that level of vibration. When the outside world begins to close in and I find my balance shifting, I take a breath, find my center and allow my higher-self to come through. In the beginning, this was more difficult. As the Kundalini ascended upward, it became much easier. Ingrained patterns can be changed. All it takes is your intent to change and your commitment to do so.

There will be times in your life that you find yourself focusing more on your growth than other times. Don't worry about this and don't push yourself. You will be led to do exactly the right thing for you. If today you feel like immersing yourself in your baseball team and foregoing your meditation, do it. You need to honor these variances. There is always an ebb and flow. Ride out the tide and let it flow back at your own pace. You will soon be motivated again and find yourself immersed in your exploration and learning.

One of the most important things to learn in balancing your inner and outer worlds is detachment. This is more easily said than done. We are so used to our old habits, the ingrained ways in which we react to people and situations, that changing the cycle requires a true commitment on your part. Detachment is viewing the world from a calm, peaceful place, without being affected by it. By recognizing the impermanence of all you see around you, it becomes easier to detach. For instance, consider your reality, that is, what you know as truth. Your reality is impermanent. Look at your life today, and think back to five years ago or two years ago or even a year ago. You're probably a very different person than you were then.

You have different values, beliefs, priorities and interests. Perhaps your job has changed, your friends, your mate or your place of residence. You have grown and matured. These are the things that make up your reality. Since they are ever changing, you can no longer consider these things permanent and you cannot count on them to remain the same. Change is the nature of the universe. If you realize this truth, what good does it do to hold onto the present and fight against the inevitable flow of change? If instead, you detach yourself from the things that are changing around you, you can "go with the flow" and stay in your peaceful center. When you feel yourself getting caught up in the emotion of the present situation, take a deep breath, mentally step back and see the flow of change around you. Allow it to flow, do not interfere. Feel the permanence and immortality of your soul. Realize the world around you is merely an illusion of separation, a temporary experience, and therefore, it does not need to affect you so profoundly.

When people think of detachment, they sometimes think of being uncaring. Nothing could be further from the truth. The Master Teacher, Jesus, is a perfect example. He was in total alignment with the Divine Source and he practiced a total detachment. He saw things from the broader perspective and was able to teach by example the power of detachment through unconditional love. Through detachment, we are free from our personal agendas. We are free to convey love and compassion to others in a way that is for their highest good, as well as ours. Detachment is love. With detachment, there is no underlying wish to control, no desire to change someone, no expectation of the outcome, only acceptance and love for the other person. Recognizing we are all free souls with free will, and recognizing that we all do what we need to for our own growth, allows you to step back and allow others the freedom they need. In doing so, you also allow yourself the freedom to grow along your own path. You allow yourself freedom from the need to gather validation, freedom from the confines of being controlled by those around you and freedom from the perceptions that have held you captive.

Through practice, you will find it easier to balance your inner and outer worlds. Realize each day brings you new opportunities for growth. The situations that arise to challenge you are helping you along your path. Do not feel discouraged when you feel the pendulum swinging too far to one side and you find yourself getting caught up in the physical world. Those around you are there by design to teach you the lessons you came here to learn. Take the opportunity to learn them.

Opening to Divine Guidance

SINCE YOU ARE READING THIS BOOK, you are on the path to connect with that which lies beyond your physical self. Whether you call this source your spiritual guide, your soul, your higher-self, the Whole, the consciousness or God, it makes no difference. In reality, they are all one. They are merely different aspects of the Whole, just as we are all one, also being different aspects that make up the Whole. Once on this path, your conscious mind begins to open and question what lies beyond and you will be directed to what you need to further your awakening. You choose the speed at which you proceed, be it slowly and cautiously or with eager acceleration. Your speed will change as you grow. Know that you are evolving and, in this, you will continue to acquire experiences to assist you in this growth.

At some point you will begin to search inward. You will look for guidance. Your guidance will come to you as you request it and you will continue to receive what you ask for. Everyone who requests this guidance will receive it. Your guidance will take whatever form is most comfortable and acceptable to you. Some people perceive guides as religious symbols such as angels, saints, Jesus, Buddha or Mohammed. Those who attach no religious intonations to the guidance will receive guidance in a form or name that is acceptable to them. Some people do not request a guide specifically, they perceive they are dealing directly with their higher-self or some other aspect of the Whole. Again, this is just a vehicle to carry you to connect with the Divine Source. Whatever you experience, know it is just right for you. It is being presented to you in just the right way for you to learn and grow.

Finding your joy is an important aspect of connecting to your soul. When you experience joy, your soul is shining through. I'm not talking about being happy because you're going on vacation, or just got a raise, or because you're getting married. Joy is what you are at your essence. Joy is a feeling of total peace within and is not dependent on outside sources. When you are joyful, you can sit in a room totally alone and a smile will come across your face for no apparent reason. You feel joy from within. It is not stimulated by any outside source. Likewise, it cannot be taken away by any outside source. Because this is so, joy is total security.

You will find joy when you find your true life purpose. When you discover something you would do for free, only you get paid for it, this is your life purpose. If you are without this in your life, try to think back to when you were a child. Remember what you wanted to do. Remember what you daydreamed about. Explore those things you always wanted to do but never got around to. Your soul is trying to steer you in the right direction. You will recognize it when it appears and you will know when you are not on the path. Seek out what gives you joy and incorporate it into your life, even if it isn't practical. Nurture this aspect of yourself. As you realign the things in your life that aren't working, you will find more and more joy creeping in. Gravitate toward that feeling and you can rest assured you are on your correct path.

I have often been asked if I were afraid of contacting a "bad spirit." Some people tell me they have begun to open to their guide, have felt the energy, but because of their fears of connecting with an evil or bad spirit they pull back and do not continue. Hollywood has indeed done a good job of indoctrinating us into what exists out there in the unknown. I will tell you that from the beginning of my experience I have never felt anything but good, positive and loving spirit guidance. Your intent is all that is required to draw to yourself what you desire. If you desire to experience the negative emotions of fear or dependency, the universe will give you what you wish. The choice is yours.

If your intent is to experience the Divine Source and you open with love in your heart, that is what you will attract to you. You needn't fear that some evil entity will swoop down and wreak havoc on your unsuspecting soul. This is a nonissue and does not warrant your concern. There is nothing evil that exists outside of you. As with everything else, we create our experiences. The experience of anything negative is totally up to you. Do not be afraid of the propaganda you have heard. For me, the issue of bad spirits is a nonissue. They simply do not exist for me. I do not allow such dark thoughts into my reality.

As you continue your search inward, you will undoubtedly be drawn to many alternative ideas and new thought processes. These changes may include changes in your personal routine, health and medical care, social interests and lifestyle and dietary changes. The following section is intended to give you a direction in which to begin. They are the things I found most helpful to incorporate into my life as I proceeded along my path. For those who have been on the path for some time you will undoubtedly find these familiar:

Relaxation or Meditation

Relaxation or meditation is vitally important as you begin to explore and understand yourself. Structure some time each day to devote to relaxation. If you are not ready for a formal meditation practice, or if the idea intimidates you, just begin by sitting quietly and relaxing. Sit and do nothing, just *be*. This does not mean reading or watching television. It is a time for your mind to turn off. Try to let all thoughts go. Focus on your breath as it goes in and out. Gradually extend the time as you feel comfortable. You will find a lot will come into your awareness as you allow the space for it to enter. Be open, and enjoy some quiet time alone with yourself. (See Chapter 19, "Meditation.")

Love Yourself

This goes along with relaxation. When you show yourself love, you treat yourself with kindness, doing what is good for you. You will allow yourself time for quiet, time for contemplation and time to pursue your interests. You need to love yourself unconditionally. Be totally accepting of all the parts of yourself. Treat your feelings with respect. Do not be critical, judgmental or impatient with yourself. Focus on your best traits and nurture those things that bring you joy. (See Chapter 18, "Loving Yourself.")

Deal with Your Issues

As I discussed in previous chapters, those issues you have not yet worked through and healed will continue to come to the surface as you continue on your path. They will demand attention so you can learn and grow from them. At some point, you will find it necessary to deal with this part of yourself before you can continue. These may be the very things that brought you to this place to begin with. Realize they have served this purpose. You may wish to consult a therapist to assist you in this process. (See Chapter 20, "Creating Peace.")

Practice Humility

Humility is a state of being that allows us to see things as they truly are because we aren't being clouded by the vision of ourselves. With humility, you will be able to focus on others and you will be open to receive the guidance as it comes. Humility gives you the peace of not having to prove yourself. When you have humility, others will be better able to accept love and guidance from you because you will be giving it unconditionally. Through humility you can transcend the superficial things and come from your heart. Those who understand greatness realize that to truly be great (not just to think you are), one must be humble.

Give Thanks

Each day I start my meditation with thanks. This can be in the form of prayer or just acknowledgment to the universe, whichever you are comfortable with. I usually start with acknowledging the people who have come into my life that I can learn from. I give thanks for the opportunity to serve others and to further evolve myself. I give thanks for my physicality, my family and the awareness I have achieved. When you state your gratitude, you are opening the door to receive more. The act of giving thanks puts you in a place of humility and places the seed of abundance in your mind. You will be focusing on what you have, not what you want. By giving thanks, you are drawing more of the same to yourself. If you want more of something, begin by giving thanks for what you already have.

State Your Intent

You need to ask for what you want. If you want to receive guidance, you will need to state what you want and why you want it. This is a cooperative venture. You are not a passive recipient. Open your heart and be honest. Don't be afraid to ask for acceleration if you feel your requests aren't being met fast enough. If your intent is pure, your request will be granted. Be aware, however, that it may not come to you in the form you asked for or expected. We do not always know what is for our highest good. Be willing to accept what comes, knowing it is exactly what you need at this point on your journey. In stating your intent to the universe you not only draw to you what you need, you open your conscious mind to accept and recognize it when it comes.

Educate Yourself

As you continue on your path, you will be searching for knowledge and information. The most common and easily accessible source of this information will be books such as this one. You will also be drawn to workshops, lectures and various events. You will learn from many teachers. Many times you will find the same thing being said in various ways. Each teacher will say something in a little different way. These differences are necessary to reach many different people. Be open to learning from all areas of your life. There is much to learn, even in the ordinary. Begin to look at the things around you in a new light. Ask yourself if there is something you can learn from each situation and each person you encounter. The more open you are to exploring new things, the faster you will evolve. Being open to new possibilities is a wonderful gift you can give yourself.

Keep a Journal

This isn't a prerequisite to connecting to your guidance; however, I feel it is an important step that can accomplish a lot of things. You needn't write daily, only when you want or need to. During times of growth, you are processing a lot of new ideas and information through your conscious mind. It is helpful to write down your insights, feelings, ideas and questions. The act of writing them down cements them into your conscious mind and forces you to focus on one thing at a time. This process helps to organize your thoughts and will serve to point you in the right direction for your continued growth. When I am trying to grasp something new, or contemplate a question, I find when I begin to write about it, the insight or answer springs into my mind. The act of clearing your mind by saving the thoughts on paper serves to open the mind for the next concept to enter.

Your Physical Body

In order for you to focus on your spiritual growth, you need to be comfortable. If your body hurts or is a burden to you, you will be preoccupied with it and unable to focus inwardly. For all your selves (body, mind, spirit) to merge you need to have balance. If your physical body is not working optimally, you will be unable to achieve a state of balance. This is not to say that those who have physical limitations or illness cannot merge with their higher selves. Each one of us needs to do the best we can with what we have. If you do the best for your body, up to your limitation, then you have done the best you can. You also need to get enough sleep and pay attention to any warning signs of illness or injury. They may be telling you to slow down and pay attention. (See Chapter 14, "The Basics— Your Physical Body.")

Diet

Drink lots of water. Water is a conductor of energy and assists your body in handling the increased energy flow from the higher vibrations. I found I began to crave water, long past the state of quenching my thirst. This was due to the high amounts of energy I feel running through my body. I noticed a distinct change in this need when I changed to a raw and living food diet. Since most fruits and vegetables have a very high water content, I found my diet took care of my need for water. As previously explained, you should transition away from all animal products and incorporate high amounts of fresh fruits and vegetables. Avoid chemical additives and try to eat organically whenever possible. These changes are a natural progression in an awakening consciousness. What may seem impossible to you as you begin your journey will seem quite natural as you grow. It is the same for the rest of your physical habits. When we get more in touch with our bodies, we naturally gravitate toward what is good for them. You may find yourself losing the taste for alcohol, junk food and sugar and you may find you actually crave foods that nourish your body. (See Chapter 16, "Divine Diet.")

Exercise

Exercise is essential. The body is meant to move and it is important to get your circulation going, to whatever extent you can manage. Aerobic activities such as walking, jogging and aerobic dance are good for the circulation and stamina and will allow for a better flow of energy. They help your body release and dispose of toxins. When I look at someone during or just after exercise, I can see their chakras actually pulsating faster and brighter. The increased breathing and circulation of aerobic activity helps to unclog our energy centers and facilitates the flow of our Divine energy. Stretching exercises, as practiced in Yoga will help with flexibility and feel wonderful after a workout. The movement will aid in your awareness of your body's physical sensations and help you to recognize its signals. We often feel alienated from our bodies. We constantly find fault with them. Learn to love and appreciate your body, no matter what shape it's in. Treat your body with respect and love. It is the vessel you have chosen to carry your spirit into physicality during this lifetime. To abuse your body is to abuse your spirit. Through this love and appreciation you will naturally begin to accept it and then change it for the better as you become more aligned with your higher-self.

C<small>HAPTE</small>R 23

The Message

T<small>HE MESSAGE CONTAINED IN THESE PAGES</small> is that you and I are the same. I have shared my thoughts, feelings and experiences so you could recognize yourself and realize the things I have experienced are possible for everyone.

You are not yet aware of your abilities or potential because you have not experienced them directly. This direct experience is possible for you when you drop your idea of limitation regarding what is possible. In reading about my experiences, you have exposed yourself to new areas and opened your mind to exploring these things for yourself. All that is needed is your intent. The rest is an escalation of natural forces beyond our current perceptual awareness. Open to this force, let it be recognized to be within you, let it be recognized to *be* you. You have nothing to fear. You must embrace the unknown in order to grow.

Know that you are truly a spiritual being. Behind all the struggles, all the doubts, all the insecurities, you are that Divine essence that is awakening to experience itself, through you. You possess such ability to love and an unending potential for compassion that there is truly nothing you cannot do. As we all awaken to our true selves, we will eliminate the problems we see around us. It is important for you to realize that these problems are surmountable. Everything is possible because within us exist all things. As you go throughout your day, touch as many people as you can, so they may touch others. Feed a stray dog, smile at a stranger, share what you have without regard for reward. You will find yourself transforming. You will find your cup overflowing as you draw from the unlimited source of universal love. You will find yourself healing because you will be connecting with the Divine within and closing the rift that has existed between you and your soul.

Above all, follow your inner guidance. Listen for that guidance every day. Recognize it in everything you do. You do have the answers. You do know what you should do. You can experience your life as you choose. Believe that this is so and your thoughts will create that experience for you. Open your mind to allow for this guidance to be heard. Do this by not second guessing everything that comes to you. You must not dismiss that "little voice" as imagination. You must not doubt yourself. You have to nurture that source that is trying to communicate with you. As you pay more and more attention to it, your focus will change and it will become clearer, much as your eyes adjust to the darkness. In a way, it is the same thing. Our inner eyes are adjusting to the darkness because we have been focusing outwardly for so long. In time, the inner light will become brighter and we will see as well inwardly as we do outwardly. This inner "seeing" brings the answers to our questions and the understanding of what to do with them.

There is a larger picture at work here. The consciousness that we all are, is collectively evolving. It is becoming more aware of itself and through that awareness there is expansion. As the collective consciousness expands, so do we, simultaneously. You must do your part. Allow for your individual expansion and seek out that which will bring it to you, so that we may know one another as ourselves and, in this, we may be healed.

Go confidently in the direction of your dreams.
Live the life you've imagined. As you simplify
your life, the laws of the universe will be simpler.
—Henry David Thoreau

Appendix
The Chakra System

CHAKRA IS A SANSKRIT WORD meaning "wheel." It refers to a spinning vortex of energy that emanates from the predominant positions around the human body. There are actually hundreds of minor chakras throughout the body, but our discussion here will focus on the seven major chakras which are located from the base of the spine to the crown of the head.

The chakras correlate to the endocrine glands and the spinal system. They regulate the energy within and outside the body for distribution throughout the nerve pathways and circulatory system. Each chakra regulates energy to a set of organs and bodily systems. When energy is blocked in a specific chakra, sets of symptoms develop in the associated organ or bodily system.

The seven major chakras represent seven different levels of spiritual development, or *spiritual awareness*. These levels are encountered, usually in order, as we live our lives. As you evolve spiritually, the lessons associated with each chakra are mastered and your soul evolves to merge with the Divine Source. It can take many lifetimes to complete this process. The speed and readiness at which you move through each chakra's lessons during your lifetime will depend greatly on the level of growth your soul has experienced prior to this incarnation.

Each chakra vibrates at a different level, creating a different color. Those with clairvoyant sight can see these colors and determine if the chakra has been mastered or if it holds emotional blockages. The energy of each chakra can be interpreted and from this information the intuitive can gain insight into the childhood of the person, their perceptions about themselves and the world, basic personality traits, fears, ability to communicate, level of intuition and spiritual understanding. The physical health can also be "read" through the energy of the chakras, as can the emotional and mental root of the illness.

The following is a summary of each chakra, its location, vibratory color, spiritual lesson and associated bodily organ or system. I have included an example to help you understand the purpose and meaning of each chakra.

First Chakra (Root Chakra)

Location:	Base of the spine
Color:	Red
Spiritual Lesson:	Lessons related to the material world, survival, instincts
Associated Area:	Sexual organs, legs and feet, pelvis area

Example:

This is the chakra where the childhood experiences are held. Our earliest ideas of ourselves and the world are held in the energy of this chakra. The energy of this chakra reveals if you felt safe, secure, loved, abandoned, neglected or unhappy as a child. These experiences carry over into the next lesson and are also apparent in the energy of the second chakra.

Second Chakra (Spleen Chakra)

Location:	Just below the navel
Color:	Orange
Spiritual Lesson:	Lessons pertaining to sexuality, work and physical desire
Associated Area:	Spleen, bladder, pancreas and kidneys

Example:

This chakra begins to develop as you leave the nest and find your own place in the world. The energy of this chakra can reveal if you are antisocial, critical of others, vain, having trouble finding your place and purpose, not trusting or suspicious. It has to do with how you relate to civilization and your place in it.

Third Chakra (Solar Plexus)

Location:	Solar Plexus
Color:	Yellow
Spiritual Lesson:	Lessons related to the ego, personality and self-esteem
Associated Area:	Digestive system, adrenal glands, stomach, liver and gall bladder

Example:

The center of self. The energy in this chakra reveals if the individual is secure in himself, has self-confidence, is comfortable in society with clear self-understanding.

Fourth Chakra (Heart Chakra)

Location:	Center of the chest
Color:	Green
Spiritual Lesson:	Lessons related to love, forgiveness and compassion
Associated Area:	Thymus gland, immune system, heart and circulatory system and assimilation of all nutrients

Example:

This chakra is the main energy center of the body. The soul is seated here. It is the major vortex for spiritual energy. Through the energy of this chakra it can be seen if you are a loving, open person or someone who is cautious and reserved. Past emotional pain is visible here, along with fears of intimacy or commitment.

Fifth Chakra (Throat Chakra)

Location:	Center of the throat
Color:	Blue
Spiritual Lesson:	Lessons related to will and self-expression

Associated Area:	Throat, thyroid, esophagus, mouth, teeth and respiratory system

Example:

The center of will, communication and creativity. This chakra becomes blocked through reluctance to express oneself. To hold in what you wish to say creates these blockages. Creativity and expression are stifled. The need to be in control and the fear of "letting go" also are reflected here.

Sixth Chakra (Third Eye)

Location:	Center of forehead, just above the eyebrows
Color:	Indigo
Spiritual Lesson:	Lessons related to mind, intuition, insight and wisdom
Associated Area:	Pituitary gland, endocrine system, immune system and brain. Sinuses, eyes, ears and the face in general.

Example:

The center of clairvoyance. When this chakra is developed, one receives intuitive visions. Dreams are received and interpreted here. When the energy of this chakra is read it reveals the degree of openness and the potential in this lifetime to fully open and experience psychic communication.

Seventh Chakra (Crown Chakra)

Location:	Crown of the head
Color:	Violet (some refer to this chakra as white energy also)
Spiritual Lesson:	Lessons related to spirituality
Associated Area:	Nervous system, skeletal system, pineal body and electrical synapses within the body

Example:

This chakra is the link to our spiritual essence. It aligns us to the higher forces of the universe. Through this chakra we can bring forth the experiences from our past lives for integration into our current lifetime. When this chakra is fully open, one has the continual experience of being one with God. The energy of this chakra reveals the level of spiritual awareness one has achieved. One's beliefs about who and what they are and the perception one has of God is held here.

End Notes

Chapter One

[1] Jung, Carl, and Hauer, J. *Kundalini Yoga.* Unpublished manuscript, 1932.

[2] Krishna, G., *Kundalini: The Evolutionary Energy in Man.* Berkeley: Shambhala, 1971.

Chapter Two

[3] TMJ is an abbreviation for Temporomandibular Joint Syndrome, which is a disorder of the temporomandibular joint of the lower jaw.

[4] A Reiki Master is someone who has achieved the final level of Reiki, which enables them to teach and initiate others into this form of energy healing.

[5] Attunement is the process in which one is opened to receive and transmit the energy.

Chapter Six

[6] This is a term for physical death, but rather than implying a finality, it indicates a transformation into another state.

Chapter Eight

[7] An ancient brotherhood, existing during the time of Christ. The Essenes' teachings were brought to light through the discovery of the Dead Sea Scrolls.

Chapter Twenty

[8] The law of cause and effect, also known as the law of action and reaction, stated, "As you sow, so shall you reap."

Bibliography

Andrews, Ted. *The Healers Manual, A Beginner's Guide to Energy Healing*. Llewellyn, 1997.

Cousens, Gabriel, M.D. *Conscious Eating*. Essene Vision Books, 1997.

Cousens, Gabriel, M.D. *Spiritual Nutrition and the Rainbow Diet*. Cassandra Press, 1986.

Myss, Caroline. *Anatomy of the Spirit*. Three Rivers Press, 1996.

Paulson, Genevieve Lewis. *Kundalini and the Chakras: A Practical Manual*. Llewellyn, 1997.

Shumsky, Susan. *Divine Revelation*. Simon and Schuster, 1996.

From Enoch to the Dead Sea Scrolls. International Biogenic Society, 1981.

The Essene Gospel of Peace, Book One. International Biogenic Society, 1981.

Recommended Reading

Contacting Your Spirit Guides

Extraordinary Guidance—How to Connect with Your Spiritual Guides by Liza M. Wiemer, published by Three Rivers Press, Crown Publishing Corp., New York, New York.

How to Meet and Work With Spirit Guides by Ted Andrews, published by Llewellyn Publications, Inc., St. Paul, Minnesota.

Opening To Channel—How to Connect With Your Guide by Sanaya Roman and Duane Packer, published by H. J. Kramer, Inc., Tiburon, California.

Psychic Ability / Mediumship

Opening Up Your Psychic Self: A Primer on Psychic Development by Petey Stevens, published by Nevertheless Press, Berkeley, California.

Proud Spirit—Lessons, Insights and Healing From The Voice of The Spirit World by Rosemary Altea, published by Eagle Brook/William Morrow.

Talking To Heaven—A Medium's Message of Life After Death by James Van Praagh, published by The Penguin Group, New York, New York.

The Eagle and The Rose by Rosemary Altea, published by Warner Books, New York, New York.

Spiritual Growth and Personal Transformation

Divine Revelation by Susan G. Shumsky, published by Simon and Schuster, New York, New York.

Kundalini and the Chakras: A Practical Manual—Evolution in This Lifetime by Genevieve Lewis Paulson, published by Llewellyn Publications, Inc., St. Paul, Minnesota.

Messengers of Light—The Angels Guide To Spiritual Growth by Terry Lynn Taylor, published by H. J. Kramer, Inc., Tiburon, California.

Personal Power Through Awareness by Sanaya Roman, published by H. J. Kramer, Inc., Tiburon, California.

Spiritual Growth—Being Your Higher-self by Sanaya Roman, published by H. J. Kramer, Inc., Tiburon, California.

Vegetarianism, Detoxification and Spiritual Diet

Awakening Our Self Healing Body—A Solution to the Health Care Crisis by Arthur M. Baker, M.A., published by Self Health Care Systems.

Becoming Vegetarian: The Complete Guide to Adapting a Healthy Vegetarian Diet by Melina Vesanto, Victoria Harrison and Brenda Davis, published by Book Publishing Company.

Conscious Eating by Gabriel Cousens, M.D., published by Essene Vision Books.

Diet for a New America by John Robbins, published by Stillpoint Publishing.

Fit for Life by Harvey and Marilyn Diamond, published by Warner Books.

Spiritual Nutrition and the Rainbow Diet by Gabriel Cousens, M.D., published by Cassandra Press, San Rafael, California.

The Sunfood Diet Success System by David Wolfe, published by Maul Brothers Publishing, San Diego, California.

The Vegetarian Handbook: Eating Right for Total Health by Gary Null, published by St. Martin's Press.

Transition to Vegetarianism—An Evolutionary Step by Rudolph Ballentine, published by The Himalayan Institute Press.

The Essenes

From Enoch to the Dead Sea Scrolls. International Biogenic Society, 1981.

The Essene Gospel of Peace, Four Book Set. International Biogenic Society, 1981.

The Essene Way—Biogenic Living. International Biogenic Society, 1989.

Szekely, Edmond Bordeaux. *The Discovery of the Essene Gospel of Peace.* International Biogenic Society, 1989.

Raw and Living Food Resources

Books:

Blatant Raw Food Propaganda by Joe Alexander. Blue Dolphin Publishing.

Conscious Eating by Gabriel Cousens, M.D. Essene Vision Books.

God's Way to Ultimate Health by Dr. George H. Malkmus. Hallelujah Acres Publishing.

Nature's First Law: The Raw-Food Diet, by Arlin, Dini, Wolfe. Maul Bros. Publishing.

Perfect Body by Roe Gallo. ProMotion Publishing.

Spiritual Nutrition and the Rainbow Diet by Gabriel Cousens, M.D. Cassandra Books.

Superior Nutrition by Herbert Shelton. Willow Publishing, Inc.

Survival into the 21st Century by Viktoras Kulvinskas, M.S. 21st Century Publications.

The Sunfood Diet Success System by David Wolfe. Maul Bros. Publishing

Raw-Food Recipe Books:

Dining in the Raw by Rita Romano. Kensington Books.

Living in the Raw, Recipes for a Healthy Lifestyle by Rose Lee Calabro. Rose Publishing.

The Raw Gourmet by Nomi Shannon. Alive Books.

Organizations:

Nature's First Law
P. O. Box 900202
San Diego, CA 92190
619-645-7282
1-800-205-2350 – orders
Web site: http://www.rawfood.com
E-mail: nature@rawfood.com
Extensive catalog of everything to do with raw food.
    Virtually every raw food book in print. Juicers, dehydrators, videos and audio tapes and raw food items.

Essene Church of Christ
P. O. Box 1113
Creswell, OR 97426
541-895-2190
 Web site: http://www.essene.org
E-mail: esseneinfo@aol.com
The Essenes advocate a raw-food vegetarian diet and
    lifestyle. The church is currently headed by Abba
    Nazariah who has been a raw-foodist for over twenty-
    three years. Information on the Essene way of life and
    raw food in general is available.

Hallelujah Acres
P. O. Box 2388
Shelby, NC 28151
704-481-1700
Hallelujah Acres was founded by Rev. George Malkmus.
    They provide publications, lectures and Health Minis-
    tries, advocating an 80 percent raw-food vegetarian diet.

Periodicals:

Living Nutrition Magazine
(Four issues per year)
Dedicated to helping health seekers learn to succeed with
    eating a natural diet of raw foods. This is an excellent
    publication. 35+ pages.
Contact is Dave Klein, 707-887-9132 or e-mail:
    dklein@living-foods.com

To subscribe: $24 / one year (four issues) or $40 / two
  years (eight issues)
Living Nutrition
P. O. Box 256
Sebastopol, CA 95473-256

Just Eat An Apple Magazine
(six issues per year)
Advocating a 100 percent raw-food diet. Providing motiva-
  tion and information, recipes and more.
800-205-2350 or email: nature@rawfood.com
To subscribe: $30 / one year or $50 / two years
Nature's First Law
P. O. Box 900202
San Diego, CA 92190

Internet Sources:

Nature's First Law:
   http://www.rawfood.com
Raw Food Online Community:
   http://www.livingfoods.com
Living Nutrition Magazine:
   http://www.living-foods-com/livingnutrition

About the Author

C HERYL BEGAN SHARING her abilities with others after the activation of her Kundalini energy in 1998. The Kundalini activation served to open her body's energy centers, allowing the emergence of the psychic abilities of clairvoyance, clairaudience and clairsentience. In addition, she is able to channel guidance directly from the Source to assist others in their healing and spiritual growth.

Currently, Cheryl provides intuitive sessions for those wishing to understand themselves and their lives. She conducts workshops teaching others to connect to their inner guidance and develop their psychic abilities. She believes we are all meant to tap into the Divine Source and bring it through to every part of our lives. She guides others to realign their lives with their spiritual essence, allowing for the natural emergence and direct experience of the Divine soul within each of us.

She is an ordained minister of the Essene New Life Church, Level II Reiki Practitioner and Animal Communicator. A vegetarian for six years, she now follows a raw and living food vegetarian diet and lifestyle. Cheryl lives in Northern California with her husband Clyde and sons, Zack and Kyle.

You can contact Cheryl by writing to her in care of Living Spirit Press or through her Web site: www.cherylstoycoff.com.